FIRE&SMOKE

FIRE & SMOKE

Get grilling with 120 delicious barbecue recipes

RICH HARRIS

Photography by Martin Poole

KYLE BOOKS

First published in Great Britain in 2016 by
Kyle Books
an imprint of Kyle Cathie Limited
192–198 Vauxhall Bridge Road
London SW1V 1DX
general.enquiries@kylebooks.com
www.kylebooks.co.uk

10 9 8 7 6 5 4 3 2 1

ISBN: 978 0 85783 350 1

A CIP catalogue record for this title is available from the British Library

Rich Harrris is hereby identified as the author of this work in accordance
with Section 77 of the Copyright, Designs and Patents Act 1988.

Text © Rich Harris 2016
Photographs © Martin Poole 2016
Design © Kyle Books 2016

Editor: Vicky Orchard
Editorial assistant: Amberley Lowis
Design: Smith & Gilmour
Photography: Martin Poole
Food styling: Rich Harris and Leonie Sooke
Props styling: Polly Webb-Wilson
Production: Nic Jones and Gemma John

Colour reproduction by F1 colour, London
Printed and bound in China by C&C Offset Printing Co., Ltd

CONTENTS

INTRODUCTION 6

CROWD-PLEASERS 16

HAND-HELD 40

FROM THE SEA 64

VEGGIES, SIDES & SLAWS 88

SAUCES, DIPS & PICKLES 118

SMOKING 132

COCKTAILS & COOLERS 158

DESSERTS 168

RESTOKE THE FIRE 186

USEFUL LINKS 202

INDEX 203

INTRODUCTION

At the faintest glimmer of sunshine, people dust off their barbecues and declare the season officially open. But why do we have this obsession with cooking outdoors? Perhaps it's the whole caveman thing, the last vestiges of the hunter-gatherer instinct that have remained with us over thousands of years of evolution. Or maybe it's simply that we love crowding around the barbecue, cracking open a few beers and delighting in the excuse to consume vast quantities of grilled meat. Whatever the reason, barbecuing has us hooked and there are now international competitions with huge sums of prize money up for grabs. It's pretty serious stuff.

Whether you're a seasoned pitmaster or have just bought your first barbecue, there should be something new and exciting for you in this book. My recipes are inspired by my travels, by my experience of working with some of the best chefs in the world on numerous TV shows and, most importantly, by my love of firing up the barbecue and getting everyone round the table for a good feed. For me, the greatest joy of outdoor cooking is the social aspect; people gather together, drinks flow and many are sat chatting around the slowly dying embers hours later. I've tried to avoid anything too cheffy, as I think barbecuing should be enjoyable rather than laborious; barbecues are often spur-of-the-moment affairs, so there are plenty of speedy recipes to suit. All the recipes have been specially designed for cooking on the barbecue because grilling over wood or charcoal is essential to the flavour of the dish; I'd never cook something on the barbecue just for the sake of it – there has to be a good reason.

I'm very aware that most people will already own a barbecue, so I'm not going to start telling you which brand to buy or that certain grills are better than others. On a very basic level, all you need is somewhere to light a fire, something to contain it and enough airflow to keep the embers glowing. Whether that's an old grill set over a couple of bricks or a top-of-the-range gas-fired beast with all the bells and whistles, it really doesn't matter; as long as you're outside, enjoying yourself and feeding your friends and family. Some of the recipes are cooked low and slow, which does require that you have some control over the cooking temperature, so a lid and vents really help. And there are a few recipes that are cooked 'dirty', which means that the food is cooked directly on the coals, so you don't even need a grill.

Our barbecue lunches or dinners always turn into a bit of a party, and a good party needs good drinks. I love craft beers and cocktails, as their big flavours stand up well to anything chargrilled, so I've included a selection of my favourite concoctions to get the occasion off to a racing start or to round off the night in style. And, in case you enjoy them a little too much, there are several brunch dishes to help clear any fuzzy heads the next morning.

Naturally, there are a lot of recipes that involve meat, and among them there are a few specialist cuts. With that in mind, I have one key piece of advice: get to know your butcher. A good butcher is more than happy to discuss the meat you're after, let you know where it's come from and prepare it the way you'd like it. If you plan on cooking one of the larger cuts such as Brisket (page 134) or Pulled Pork (page 142), give your butcher a bit of notice so that they can order in what you need. You pay the price for the weight of the meat, not for the preparation, so asking for a jointed chicken, for instance, isn't going to cost you more and will save you time and cut fingers. The same goes for fish.

There will be some familiar recipes and some twists on classics, but the main focus is getting you to make the most from outdoor cooking, trying some exciting flavour combinations and ultimately taking your whole barbecue experience to the next level.

TYPES OF BARBECUE/SMOKER

If you've bought this book, it's likely that you already own a barbecue, and in any case there are so many different sorts on offer, but here are a few words of guidance on the main types and what you can achieve with them.

KETTLE BARBECUE

Perhaps the most common type of barbecue, these are relatively inexpensive, come in various sizes depending on how many you're feeding (or how popular you are) and are easy to set up and maintain. They are perfect for traditional grilling, and if they have top and bottom vents they can be used for low and slow cooking. They also make great vessels for cold smoking (see page 12).

KAMADO GRILL

This heavy-duty, ceramic-lined grill is the ultimate all-rounder. Depending on how you set it up, the kamado can be used for low and slow cooking as well as traditional grilling, and even turns into a pizza oven. These are well-sealed units with great insulation, so the fuel burns longer and slower therefore enabling you to cook for hours on just a few handfuls of charcoal and wood. Top and bottom vents allow for really accurate temperature control. They're at the higher end of the price range as far as anything coal-fired goes, but definitely a worthwhile investment if you're serious about grilling.

OFFSET BARREL SMOKER

These rely solely on indirect heat, so are perfect for cooking anything low and slow. The design means that the fuel is housed in a separate compartment, allowing the heat and smoke to flow through the cooking chamber, circulate around the food and then drift out through the chimney. Again, vents allow you to regulate the temperature. The main benefit is that it's easy to top up the fuel for longer cooking without disturbing the meat. They can also be used for traditional direct grilling (see page 11) by building the fire directly below the cooking grates in the smoking compartment.

BULLET SMOKER

This upright smoker has multiple compartments, allowing you to smoke several different items at once. Many come as modular units so that they can be expanded or reduced in size depending on how many people you're feeding. They can also be set up for traditional direct grilling (see page 11) and the shape means that they're handy if you're short on space.

GAS BARBECUE

Great for their convenience factor, many gas grills now come with cool features like electric rotisseries and under-counter fridges. Temperature control is easy, and as long as you have a full bottle, you can cook for ages with little fuss. There is the argument that gas barbecues don't produce the same flavour as cooking over charcoal and wood, which I'd agree with, but you can buy smoking boxes so that you can add flavour with wood chips (see page 12).

DISPOSABLE FOIL TRAY BARBECUE

Don't. Just don't.

DIRECT VS INDIRECT GRILLING

Throughout the recipes in this book you'll see that dishes are either cooked over direct or indirect heat, or occasionally a combination of both.

DIRECT GRILLING

Direct grilling is exactly what it says on the tin: the grill is positioned directly over the heat source. This is what you probably think of as traditional barbecuing; it's a way of cooking hard and fast, giving meat, fish and vegetables an intense chargrilled flavour. The biggest mistake people make is treating a barbecue like a griddle pan or frying pan and leaving a piece of meat sitting in one position, which can either lead to it burning or taking too long to cook. Whether the heat is blisteringly high or relatively moderate, the most important point is to keep things moving. Without getting too scientific, if the heat is high and you leave a piece of meat cooking without moving it, the outside will be overcooked and the centre raw. By regularly turning you'll ensure that it's cooked evenly. People worry that they'll lose that lovely charred crust, but that will come towards the end of cooking, trust me. Equally, if the heat is fairly moderate, it's just as important to keep the food moving. For example, if you have a thick slab of lamb sizzling away, the bars directly underneath it will be lower in temperature than the empty areas of the grill, as they are exposed to the coals underneath without anything getting in the way. Rather than simply turning that lovely piece of lamb in the same spot, turn and then move it to another part of the grill and you'll get a deep char on the meat, resulting in even better flavour.

INDIRECT GRILLING/ HOT SMOKING

Indirect grilling requires a different set-up to allow for low and slow cooking. The heat source and the food need to be separated and the heat diffused to prevent the food from cooking too quickly. Airflow is also important; if you want to maintain a really low temperature (about 125°C is ideal), the air intake at the bottom of the barbecue and exhaust at the top need to be kept to a minimum. Ensure that neither is ever fully closed, though, otherwise you'll starve the fire of oxygen and it will quickly go out.

The set-up for the most commonly owned kettle barbecue is still fairly straightforward. Build your fire as usual, and when the coals are glowing white, push everything to one side. Lay a foil tray filled with water next to the coals and set the grill over the top. Lay another water-filled tray on the grill directly above the glowing coals. The food goes on the empty half of the grill. Then it's just a case of closing the lid and adjusting the top and bottom vents to maintain a steady temperature. If your barbecue isn't fitted with a temperature gauge, you can use a cheap oven thermometer or hang a digital probe thermometer in the main cooking chamber.

Depending on the type of charcoal you're using, and the type of barbecue or smoker, you may need to top up the fuel during cooking. This is where a chimney starter comes in really handy as it allows you to get the coals to the right temperature before topping them up. Don't try to add 'cold' charcoal or wood straight to the fire as their initial burn will give off acrid smoke which will taint the flavour of the food.

Cooking low and slow over indirect heat will naturally smoke whatever you're cooking, but if you want to increase that smoky flavour, you can add hardwood chunks to your charcoal so that they gently smoulder during the cook. Do ensure the wood is properly charred and only gently smouldering before you start cooking; if thick smoke is billowing out it'll give the food a nasty acrid taste. The meat needs to be gently caressed by the smoke, not shrouded in a dense cloud.

For faster hot-smoked recipes, you can use smoking pellets that can be applied directly to the coals, or smoking chips that will need to be soaked in warm water for about 30 minutes to stop them from igniting.

COLD SMOKING

Cold smoking is altogether a different kettle of fish and I've only touched on it in a few recipes. The main difference, fairly obviously, is the temperature of the cooking environment. To cold smoke safely, you need the interior of the cooking chamber (i.e. your barbecue or smoker) to remain below 25°C to inhibit bacteria growth and stop the food from cooking. In order to keep the heat to a minimum, and to ensure a long, even smoke, your best option is smoking wood. There are plenty of great online suppliers (see Useful Links, page 202) that stock a variety of different woods in dust form. To ensure that the wood dust burns slowly and evenly, I use a ProQ Cold Smoke Generator. It's basically a spiral-shaped metal frame that you pack with wood dust and it burns for up to 10 hours. I place mine in the bottom of my barbecue, open the vents slightly and then lay whatever I want to smoke on the grill above. I strongly advise you not to cold smoke outdoors in the height of summer; the barbecue will get too hot in the sunshine and you'll end up with something halfway between hot smoked and cold smoked that will almost definitely make you unwell.

 DIRECT GRILLING

 INDIRECT GRILLING

 COLD SMOKING

 FRESH UNCOOKED

 DIRTY COOKING

 OVEN/HOB COOKING

FUEL

Good fuel is essential and can really make the difference between a good barbecue and a great one. The best way to think of it is to treat the fuel you use as an ingredient in your cooking. It may sound a bit ridiculous, but when you consider that something as delicious as brisket is made up of just three ingredients, beef, salt and pepper, all that deep, sweet, smoky flavour relies entirely on the charcoal and wood you use.

CHARCOAL AND FIRELIGHTERS

I always use sustainably sourced lumpwood charcoal, which gives a great flavour and, with the right temperature control, will burn away for hours on end. The cheap, instant-lighting stuff can be full of nasty chemicals to help it burn longer, chemicals that you really don't want to end up in your food. For the same reason, I always use natural firelighters.

WOODS

As well as charcoal, I like to use a range of hardwoods, either as logs, chunks, chips or pellets, depending on the length of the cook. Different woods will impart different flavours to the finished product, so I'd encourage you to find a local supplier and have a play around. I've used the following combinations of wood and ingredients:

Apple: chicken and pork
Cherry: beef and pork
Hickory: beef, pork, poultry
Maple: pork and poultry
Mesquite: beef and chicken
Oak: beef, chicken and fish
Olive: beef, pork and lamb
Orange: chicken, pork and fish

BARBECUING KIT

The beauty of outdoor cooking is that, once you have taken possession of a half-decent barbecue, you only need a few essential tools:

Digital probe thermometer: There are loads of these on the market and some can be linked to a smartphone. I use a wireless probe, which is inexpensive and means that I can leave meat cooking outside and keep an eye on its progress without having to stand by the barbecue for hours.

Long matches: Because nobody likes burnt fingers.

Chimney starter: This will help to get your barbecue fuel going quickly and efficiently, and is useful for topping it up during long cooks.

Heavy-duty black rubber gloves: For handling charcoal and making the neighbours think that you're a bit sinister.

Old, clean tea towels: To help with handling large pieces of meat during cooking.

Foil trays or old roasting trays: To hold food as it cooks or for use as water trays for indirect cooking; foil trays are reusable, and both save ruining your nice non-stick trays.

Spray bottle: For spritzing meat to keep it moist during cooking, and to remove any excess smoke particles (which can make the meat taste a little bitter). Also handy to fill with oil for spraying the bars on the grill.

A couple of old, heavy-based saucepans: For cooking sauces on the grill.

The list below is really useful if you've got a digital probe thermometer. It shows the temperature at which you need to remove the meat from the grill, and the final temperature you're looking for after resting. Stick with these and you can't go wrong.

BEEF AND LAMB

Rare
Temperature out of the barbecue: 50°C
Temperature after resting: 56°C

Medium rare
Temperature out of the barbecue: 56°C
Temperature after resting: 62°C

Medium
Temperature out of the barbecue: 62°C
Temperature after resting: 68°C

Well done
Temperature out of the barbecue: 68°C
Temperature after resting: 72°C

PORK

Medium
Temperature out of the barbecue: 60°C
Temperature after resting: 70°C

Well done
Temperature out of the barbecue: 70°C
Temperature after resting: 80°C

CHICKEN AND TURKEY
Temperature out of the barbecue: 68°C
Temperature after resting: 75°C

CROWD-PLEASERS

BEEF SHORT RIBS with SMOKED BEER and ROOT VEGETABLE SLAW

Short ribs are a fantastic cut of beef but need to be cooked low and slow. The result is beautifully tender, intensely flavoured beef with a rich barbecue sauce. You can cook the ribs up to the chilling stage a day ahead, so that when your guests turn up the ribs just need to be heated through and basted with the sauce. I normally used a dark, porter-style beer as the toasted malt flavour worked really well with the beef. However, my butcher Will recently introduced me to an amazing German smoked beer called Original Schlenkerla Smokebeer, which is made using toasted malt smoked over birch wood; it's definitely worth trying to get hold of a bottle if you can.

SERVES 4 | PREP TIME: 40 MINUTES PLUS CHILLING | COOK TIME: 5 HOURS

4 large beef short ribs, weighing approx. 450g each
1 carrot, peeled and roughly chopped
1 celery stick, roughly chopped
1 onion, roughly chopped
6 garlic cloves, bashed
4 star anise
500ml smoked beer, porter or other dark beer
500ml beef stock
150ml Quick Sharp Barbecue Sauce (page 128) or other tangy barbecue sauce

FOR THE SLAW
2 parsnips, peeled and coarsely grated
2 carrots, peeled and coarsely grated
1 red onion, coarsely grated
½ small celeriac, peeled and coarsely grated
1 teaspoon fine sea salt
½ teaspoon caster sugar
juice of 1 lemon
3 tablespoons Mayonnaise (page 131)
2 teaspoons grain mustard
2 tablespoons finely chopped chives
sea salt and freshly ground black pepper

gherkins, to serve

Preheat the oven to 150°C/gas mark 2. Lay the ribs in a large roasting tin with the vegetables, garlic and star anise. Bring the beer and stock to the boil in a saucepan, then pour over the ribs. Cover the tin tightly with foil and cook for 4 hours. Set aside to cool. Once the liquid has cooled to room temperature, remove the ribs and transfer to a tray or large plate. Cover with clingfilm and chill in the fridge for 2 hours or overnight if possible.

Strain the liquid from the roasting tin into a clean pan and skim off as much fat as possible. Bring to the boil and then reduce by two-thirds until thickened and glossy. Remove from the heat and whisk in the barbecue sauce.

Preheat the barbecue for direct grilling (see page 11).

Meanwhile, combine all the slaw ingredients in a large bowl, season to taste and set aside. Unwrap the ribs, brush with the sauce and then grill for 10 minutes, turning and basting with the sauce regularly. Remove the ribs from the heat, give them a final brush then serve with the slaw, the remaining sauce and gherkins on the side.

DRY-RUBBED SIRLOIN of BEEF with BURNT ONIONS

This is an impressive dish to serve to a crowd and a far easier way to cook beef than juggling loads of steaks on the barbecue. By starting the beef off over indirect heat, you'll have beautifully tender, evenly cooked meat that just needs a quick flash over direct heat to finish. Serve thickly sliced with the burnt onions and Béarnaise Sauce (page 131), or thinly sliced and piled into baps with the onions and some Chimichurri (page 128).

SERVES 8 | PREP TIME: 30 MINUTES | COOK TIME: 2 HOURS 20 MINUTES–2 HOURS 50 MINUTES PLUS RESTING

2kg boneless sirloin joint

FOR THE RUB
1½ tablespoons freshly ground black pepper
1 tablespoon fine sea salt
1 tablespoon hot smoked paprika
1 tablespoon dark brown soft sugar
1 teaspoon ground allspice
1 teaspoon dried rosemary

FOR THE BURNT ONIONS
1 garlic bulb
3 red onions, peeled but roots left intact
3 sweet white onions, peeled but roots left intact
1 bunch of fat spring onions, trimmed
4 banana shallots, peeled and halved lengthways
3 sprigs of thyme, leaves chopped
1 tablespoon extra virgin olive oil
2 tablespoons sherry vinegar
1 tablespoon grain mustard
pinch of caster sugar

Béarnaise Sauce (page 131) or Chimichurri (page 128), to serve

Preheat the barbecue for indirect grilling (see page 11). Score the fat on top of the beef joint at regular intervals, taking care not to cut through to the meat. Combine all the rub ingredients in a small bowl. The next step can get messy, so lay the beef in a large tray before covering it with the rub; really work it into the flesh. Push a digital probe thermometer into the centre of the beef.

Lift the beef out of the tray and lay fat-side up on the grill, then sit the garlic bulb next to it. Close the lid and cook for 2–2½ hours or until the thermometer reads 50°C (it will climb another 6°C during the resting stage; see my cooking temperature guide on page 15). Remove the garlic and beef from the grill and adjust the barbecue for direct grilling (see page 11).

Sear the beef for about 10 minutes until lightly charred, then remove from the heat and leave to rest for 20 minutes.

While the beef is resting, prepare the burnt onions. Cut all the onions into thick wedges through the root; this will stop them from falling apart as they cook. Lay on the grill with the spring onions and shallots and grill for 10 minutes until charred and softened, turning occasionally. Remove the onions and set aside until cool enough to handle. Trim away the roots, and separate into individual leaves. Roughly chop the spring onions.

Cut the top off the garlic bulb and squeeze the soft flesh into a large bowl. Add the thyme, oil, vinegar, mustard, sugar and any juices from the resting beef. Stir to combine, then add the charred onions and toss to coat.

Carve the beef and serve with the burnt onions, Béarnaise Sauce or Chimichurri.

TOMAHAWK STEAKS
with BLUE CHEESE BUTTER

A tomahawk steak is a thick-cut rib-eye with the whole rib bone still attached; a long-handled côte de boeuf, if you will. It's an impressive way of serving up a sharing steak, and cooking the beef on the bone keeps it moist and adds loads of flavour. It's a little specialist, so give your butcher some notice when ordering. Feel free to serve a few sauces such as Béarnaise (page 131), Chimichurri (page 128) and Salsa Verde (page 129) alongside.

SERVES 4 | PREP TIME: 5 MINUTES | COOK TIME: 15–20 MINUTES PLUS RESTING

2 dry-aged tomahawk steaks, weighing 800–900g each
fine sea salt

FOR THE BLUE CHEESE BUTTER
125g strong soft blue cheese (I use Barkham Blue but Gorgonzola Piccante also works well)
100g unsalted butter, softened

TO SERVE
Buttermilk Onion Rings (page 98)
Mac 'n' Cheese (page 99)

Remove the steaks from the fridge 30 minutes before cooking and preheat the barbecue for direct grilling (see page 11). Salt the steaks generously and grill for 15–20 minutes, depending on how you like your steak, turning regularly. Remove from the heat and set aside to rest for 10 minutes.

Meanwhile, crumble the cheese into a large bowl and gradually beat in the softened butter until combined, leaving a few crumbs of cheese still showing.

Run a sharp knife along the bone to separate it from the meat. Carve the steak into thick slices and serve with the blue cheese butter along with Buttermilk Onion Rings and Mac 'n' Cheese.

SPICED LEG of LAMB

People often butterfly a leg of lamb to barbecue it, but invariably you'll have one thicker end, so the thinner pieces will be overcooked by the time the thicker part is ready. There will also be a couple of large pockets of fat that will cause the coals to flare and can scorch the meat. I separate the lamb leg into its component muscles and cook them individually, starting with the largest. You'll have more control over the cooking and the marinade will cover more of the meat.

SERVES 6 | PREP TIME: 30 MINUTES PLUS CHILLING | COOK TIME: 15 MINUTES

1 boneless leg of lamb,
   weighing approx. 2.2kg

FOR THE MARINADE
2 teaspoons fennel seeds
2 teaspoons cumin seeds
2 teaspoons coriander seeds
1 teaspoon chilli flakes
1 teaspoon sweet paprika
1 teaspoon fine sea salt
5 garlic cloves, crushed
thumb-sized piece of fresh
   ginger, peeled and grated
olive oil

TO SERVE
Baba Ganoush (page 120)
Hot Sauce (page 128)
Tabbouleh (page 106)

Lay the lamb flat on a large chopping board and carefully work your way around it, separating it into individual muscles; you should be able to do most of the work with your hands, using a sharp knife to make the final cuts. Depending on how the bone was removed, you should end up with five or six individual pieces. Trim away any large white pieces of fat and any sinew, then put the lamb into a large bowl.

Tip the whole spices into a dry frying pan and toast over a medium heat for a couple of minutes until they begin to smell nutty. Tip into a pestle and mortar and grind to a fine powder. Add the chilli flakes, paprika, salt, garlic and ginger and pound until smooth. Work in enough oil to make a loose paste, then pour over the lamb and toss to coat evenly. Cover with clingfilm and chill in the fridge for at least 4 hours or overnight if possible.

Remove the lamb from the fridge 30 minutes before cooking and preheat the barbecue for direct grilling (see page 11). Start off by cooking the larger pieces – they'll take about 15 minutes – and gradually add the smaller pieces as you go. The idea is for all the lamb to be cooked at roughly the same time. Keep turning the lamb as it cooks. As each piece of lamb is ready, transfer it to a warm plate to rest. Carve the lamb against the grain and serve with Baba Ganoush, Hot Sauce and Tabbouleh.

DIRTY CHOPS with ROSEMARY BUTTER and PICKLED FENNEL

'Dirty' cooking simply refers to cooking directly on the coals. With that in mind, it's really important to use natural firelighters and decent lumpwood charcoal, free from any chemicals or other nasty surprises. Laying the meat straight on the coals results in incredible flavour and, importantly, the meat doesn't burn because there's no oxygen between the surface of the coals and the meat so it can't catch fire. The only tricky part is the skin on the pork chops – make sure that it's hanging off the edge of the coals so that it cooks indirectly (the skin will cook far quicker than the rest of the chop). This also works brilliantly with thick-cut steaks and whole vegetables. Just keep a brush to hand to dust off any loose flecks of charcoal.

SERVES 4 | PREP TIME: 15 MINUTES PLUS CHILLING | COOK TIME: 20 MINUTES

4 thick-cut pork chops,
   skin on
fine sea salt

FOR THE PICKLED FENNEL
1 large fennel bulb, quartered,
   cored and finely sliced
1 teaspoon fine sea salt
200ml boiling water
150ml white wine vinegar
4 tablespoons caster sugar

FOR THE ROSEMARY BUTTER
4 sprigs of rosemary,
   leaves chopped
good pinch of sea salt flakes
75g unsalted butter, at room
   temperature

A few hours before cooking, stack the pork chops skin-side up in a roasting tin. Boil a kettle of water and carefully pour the just-boiled water over the skin. Pat the chops dry, then lay them on a wire rack, uncovered, and chill in the fridge for 2–3 hours.

To make the pickled fennel, put the fennel and salt into a large bowl and toss to combine, then gently knead together for 5 minutes until softened. Combine the boiling water, vinegar and sugar in a jug and stir until the sugar has dissolved. Pour over the fennel and leave to cool to room temperature. The fennel will be ready to eat straight away, but tastes even better if you make it a day ahead, storing it in the fridge once it has cooled.

To make the rosemary butter, put the rosemary leaves into a mortar with the salt and grind to a fine paste with a pestle. Gradually work the butter in until you have a vibrant green paste. Spoon into a bowl, cover with clingfilm and chill until needed.

Preheat the barbecue and remove the grill. Meanwhile, remove the chops from the fridge and season with plenty of salt. When the coals are glowing white, push them to one side of the barbecue. Lay the chops directly on the coals; the idea is to rest the meat on the coals but leave the skin hanging off the edge. This way you'll get delicious crackling and perfectly cooked meat. Cook the chops for 7–8 minutes, turning occasionally. Remove from the coals, give them a quick dust to remove any ash then set aside to rest for 5 minutes. Serve with the pickled fennel and rosemary butter on the side.

SZECHUAN SMOKED PIG CHEEKS
with PLUM KETCHUP

The cheeks are often the best part of an animal; besides pig cheeks, think ox cheeks and even cod or monkfish cheeks. The hardest-working parts of an animal are always the tastiest, and as pigs spend their days chomping, their cheeks have a pretty decent workout. Szechuan pepper adds an addictive heat and tingly sensation that works brilliantly with the smoky pork. I serve these really simply, roughly torn into chunks with a dollop of homemade plum ketchup for dipping. Sticky finger food at its finest.

SERVES 4 | PREP TIME: 20 MINUTES | COOK TIME: 3 HOURS PLUS RESTING

12 pig cheeks, trimmed
  of sinew
2 tablespoons Szechuan
  peppercorns
1 tablespoon fine sea salt
1 tablespoon sweet paprika
100ml apple juice
100ml cider vinegar

FOR THE PLUM KETCHUP
  (makes 600ml)
600g ripe plums, stoned
  and quartered
2 ripe tomatoes, roughly
  chopped
1 small onion, finely chopped
1 garlic clove, crushed
2 dried red chillies, stalks
  removed
3 star anise
1 cinnamon stick
350ml cider vinegar
200g demerara sugar
50g black treacle
2 teaspoons fine sea salt

You will need a large handful of wood chips (see page 12), soaked in warm water for 30 minutes.

Preheat the barbecue or smoker for indirect grilling (see page 11). Lay the pig cheeks in a foil tray. Pound the Szechuan peppercorns with the salt and paprika to a fine powder with a pestle and mortar. Sprinkle over the pork in an even layer, ensuring that each piece is coated in the rub. Set the tray on the grill, close the lid and cook for an hour. Combine the apple juice and vinegar in a spray bottle, give the cheeks a good spritz then cook for a further hour.

Remove the tray from the barbecue or smoker, cover tightly with foil and return to the barbecue or smoker for a further hour.

Meanwhile, make the plum ketchup. Combine all the ingredients in a heavy-based pan and bring to the boil. Reduce to a simmer and cook for an hour, stirring occasionally, until the fruit has broken down and the mixture is thick and jammy. Remove from the heat, retrieve the star anise and cinnamon stick and leave to cool.

Pour the plum mixture into a liquidiser and blend until smooth. This makes more than you'll need for this recipe, so pour any leftover ketchup into a sterilised jar or bottle, seal and keep in the fridge for up to 2 months.

Remove the pork from the heat and leave to rest for 10 minutes, then tear into chunks and serve with the plum ketchup.

TIP: I'm not a big fan of cheats and shortcuts when it comes to cooking, but here's one of my very few exceptions to the rule: if you're cooking for a small group, or just short on time, you can use pig cheeks for my Pulled Pork recipe (page 142).

STICKY CHILLI PORK BELLY
with RICE NOODLE SALAD

Barbecued pork belly has a crispy, charred exterior giving way to beautifully soft meat. Once grilled, I quickly toss the hot pork in my Sweet Chilli Sauce (page 123), which melts and glazes the meat. The sauce is so easy to make and definitely worth the effort, as shop-bought ones can be overly sugary and lacking in chilli heat.

SERVES 6 | PREP TIME: 25 MINUTES PLUS COOLING | COOK TIME: 3 HOURS 10 MINUTES

3 carrots, peeled and
   halved lengthways
3 celery sticks
2 onions, quartered
4 star anise
150ml dark soy sauce
2.5kg piece of skinless,
   boneless pork belly (see tip)
6 tablespoons Sweet Chilli
   Sauce (page 123)

FOR THE SALAD
150g dried rice vermicelli
3 red bird's eye chillies,
   finely chopped
1 garlic clove, crushed
juice of 3 limes
3 tablespoons fish sauce
2 tablespoons palm sugar
6 Thai shallots, finely sliced
½ cucumber, peeled,
   deseeded and finely sliced
1 large bunch of mint,
   leaves torn
1 large bunch of coriander,
   leaves torn
1 large bunch of Thai sweet
   basil, leaves torn

Preheat the oven to 160°C/gas mark 3. Arrange the carrots, celery, onions and star anise in the bottom of a large roasting tray and pour over the soy sauce. Lay the pork on top and pour over enough boiling water to just cover. Cover the tray tightly with foil and cook for 3 hours, carefully turning the pork halfway through cooking. Remove from the oven and leave to cool completely.

Remove the pork from the liquid and lay on a clean baking tray. Lay a second tray on top and wrap tightly in clingfilm. Transfer to the fridge and sit a heavy weight on top (I use a small cast-iron pan, but a few tins of beans will do). Chill overnight.

Preheat the barbecue for direct grilling (see page 11). For the salad, put the noodles in a large bowl, cover with boiling water and leave to stand for 10 minutes or according to the packet instructions until just soft. Drain and refresh under cold running water. Combine the chillies, garlic, lime juice, fish sauce and palm sugar in a bowl and stir until the sugar has dissolved. Add the noodles and toss to coat.

Unwrap the pork and use a sharp knife to cut it into thick slabs. Grill for 10 minutes, turning regularly, until crisp and golden all over. Chop the pork into bite-sized chunks, then transfer to a large bowl or roasting tray, add the sweet chilli sauce and toss to coat. Toss the shallots, cucumber and herbs through the noodle salad and serve with the pork.

TIP: Ask your butcher to remove the skin from the pork belly and take it home with you. If you want to really jazz up this dish, roast the skin in a really hot oven until crisp, then break into shards and scatter over the salad.

PORCHETTA

During my last couple of trips to Italy, in and around Umbria, Tuscany and Marché, I've become completely hooked on their famous roast pork. Like so many things, as soon as it's on your radar you start to notice it everywhere; at markets, in town squares and at the roadside, porchetta vendors seemed to be everywhere. Unlike our traditional hog roasts, porchetta tends to be served cold then thinly sliced and stuffed into a crusty white roll with a generous sprinkling of salt. This is perhaps the only occasion I'd cook pork and not worry about crackling; it's the low, slow cooking over gently smouldering wood that's so important. I've given approximate weights for the pork here as it'll vary slightly depending on the breed of pig; the best thing to do is speak to your butcher. Ask for a large piece of pork belly and a piece of loin the right size to be rolled up inside.

SERVES 10–12 | PREP TIME: 25 MINUTES | COOK TIME: 5½–6 HOURS PLUS RESTING

approx. 4kg piece of
   boneless pork belly,
   skin scored
approx. 2kg piece of
   boneless pork loin
fine sea salt

FOR THE FILLING
2 fennel bulbs
1 garlic bulb, cloves
   separated and peeled
3 tablespoons olive oil
3 tablespoons coarsely
   ground black pepper
3 tablespoons fennel seeds
2 tablespoons fine sea salt
2 teaspoons chilli flakes
6 sprigs of rosemary,
   leaves picked

crusty white bread rolls, to serve

For the filling, roughly chop the fennel bulbs and put into a food processor with the garlic, then pulse until finely chopped. Heat the oil in a frying pan, add the fennel and fry gently for 15 minutes until softened. Add the remaining filling ingredients and fry for a further couple of minutes, then set aside to cool slightly. Tip into a food processor, blend to a rough paste and leave to cool.

Preheat the barbecue for indirect grilling (see page 11). Lay the pork belly out skin-side down and spread the filling mixture over in an even layer. Lay the loin at one end and roll the belly up tightly; this can get a bit messy, so an extra pair of hands is useful here. Tie tightly with butcher's string at regular intervals to hold the pork together and then salt the skin generously. Lay on the grill, close the lid and cook for 5–5½ hours. Set aside to rest for at least 30 minutes before removing the string and carving. Serve in crusty white bread rolls.

JERK CHICKEN

Proper jerk chicken should be succulent, aromatic and face-numbingly spicy. There are
a few key ingredients that make it a proper jerk: allspice, black pepper and Scotch Bonnet
chillies. I use four whole Scotch Bonnets, which gives a pretty serious kick to the chicken,
but use a couple more if you're feeling brave.

SERVES 6 | PREP TIME: 20 MINUTES PLUS MARINATING | COOK TIME: 45–50 MINUTES PLUS RESTING

1 large free-range chicken,
    weighing approx. 2kg, jointed
1 tablespoon allspice berries
1 tablespoon black peppercorns
10 cloves
1 teaspoon ground nutmeg
6 sprigs of thyme, leaves picked
2 bay leaves
6 garlic cloves, peeled
thumb-sized piece of
    fresh ginger, peeled
    and roughly chopped
1 bunch of spring onions,
    roughly chopped
4 Scotch Bonnet chillies,
    stalks removed
4 tablespoons white
    wine vinegar
2 teaspoons dark brown
    soft sugar
1 teaspoon fine sea salt

lime wedges, to serve

You will need a large handful
of wood chips (see page 12),
soaked in warm water for
30 minutes.

Slash the skin on the chicken drumsticks and thighs at regular
intervals, then put in a large bowl. Grind the allspice berries,
peppercorns and cloves to a fine powder using a pestle and
mortar or a spice grinder. Tip the ground spices and the
remaining ingredients into a food processor and blend until
smooth. Pour over the chicken and toss to coat, cover with
clingfilm and leave to marinate in the fridge for 3–4 hours
or overnight if possible.

Remove the chicken from the fridge 30 minutes before
cooking, preheat the barbecue for indirect grilling (see page 11)
and add the soaked wood chips. Lay the legs, thighs and wings
on the grill, close the lid and grill for 20 minutes, turning after
10 minutes. Add the breast pieces to the grill and continue to
cook for a further 20 minutes. Remove the chicken from the
grill and adjust the barbecue for direct grilling (see page 11).
Once the barbecue has come up to temperature, return the
chicken to the grill and cook for 5–10 minutes until the skin
is crispy and lightly charred.

To check that the chicken is cooked, insert a small sharp
knife into one of the drumsticks; the meat closest to the bone
should be cooked through with no traces of pink and the juices
should run clear. Set aside to rest for a few minutes then serve
with lime wedges.

SPATCHCOCK CHICKEN
with CHERMOULA

North African Chermoula is often used as either a marinade or sauce for fish. However, I think it goes beautifully with chicken and didn't want to settle for marinade *or* sauce; I wanted both. Preserved lemons are really worth hunting down as they add a savoury, fragrant bitterness that works beautifully with the crisp, charred chicken skin.

SERVES 4–6 | PREP TIME: 20 MINUTES PLUS MARINATING | COOK TIME: 40–50 MINUTES

1 large free-range chicken, weighing approx. 2kg

FOR THE CHERMOULA
4 preserved lemons or coarsely grated zest of 2 unwaxed lemons
3 garlic cloves, peeled
100ml olive oil
juice of 2 lemons
1 tablespoon sweet paprika
1 teaspoon chilli flakes
1 teaspoon fine sea salt, plus extra to season the sauce
2 tablespoons cumin seeds, toasted
100g fresh coriander
freshly ground black pepper

You will need 2 metal or wooden skewers; if you're using wooden ones, soak them in warm water for at least an hour.

Lay the chicken breast-side down on a chopping board with the neck end facing away from you. Take a pair of poultry shears or sturdy kitchen scissors and cut to one side of the parson's nose, cutting all the way down the backbone. Make the same cut on the other side then discard the strip of bone you've removed. Turn the chicken over on the board, lay your hand flat across the breasts and push down firmly to flatten out. Transfer to a large dish or roasting tray and set aside.

Halve the chermoula ingredients; you need half for the marinade, and half for the sauce. For the marinade, quarter the lemons and scrape away the flesh and seeds then roughly chop into a food processor. Add the remaining marinade ingredients and blend until smooth. Pour over the chicken and ensure that all of the bird is covered, working some the marinade under the skin on the breasts. Cover with clingfilm and transfer to the fridge for a couple of hours or overnight if possible.

Remove the chicken from the fridge 30 minutes before cooking and preheat the barbecue for direct grilling (see page 11). Lay the chicken breast-side up on a board and insert a skewer diagonally through the chicken; the aim is to thread it through the leg, thigh and breast and then out the other side. Repeat with a second skewer through the other side of the chicken to form an 'X'; this will keep the bird flat, helping it to cook evenly.

Lay the chicken on the grill breast-side up and cook for 40–50 minutes, turning every 10 minutes. To check that the chicken is cooked, insert a sharp knife into the thickest part of the thigh. No pink flesh and juices running clear? The chook is cooked. Transfer to a board and set aside to rest for 15 minutes while you make the chermoula sauce.

Prepare the preserved lemons as for the marinade, but finely chop the skin into a bowl with the remaining garlic, oil, lemon juice, paprika, chilli flakes and salt. Grind the remaining cumin seeds to a coarse powder with a pestle and mortar and add. Finely chop the remaining coriander, stir in and season to taste.

Remove the skewers from the chicken, carve into chunks and arrange on a serving platter. Scrape up any resting juices, pour over the chicken and serve with the chermoula sauce.

CHICKEN and SALT

There are three very straightforward steps that lead to incredible chicken. The first is to dry-brine the chicken in salt; as well as seasoning the meat, this starts to break down some of the muscle fibres, which would ordinarily contract during cooking and force moisture out. The second stage is to slowly cook the chicken in an oven to retain any roasting juices, which create a delicious glaze. The final step is to crisp and lightly char the chicken skin on the barbecue before glazing in the reserved roasting juices. It's really easy and you can cook a large batch of chicken with very little fuss; perfect if you're feeding a hungry crowd.

SERVES 4–6 | PREP TIME: 20 MINUTES PLUS CHILLING | COOK TIME: 1 HOUR

1 large free-range,
   corn-fed chicken,
   weighing approx. 2kg
fine sea salt
pinch of sea salt flakes

The day before you plan to barbecue, joint the chicken (or ask your butcher to do it for you). Sprinkle a good pinch of fine sea salt over the chicken in an even layer, then transfer to a large plastic food bag and seal tightly. Chill in the fridge overnight.

The next day, preheat the oven to 120°C/gas mark ½ and remove the chicken from the fridge. After 30 minutes the chicken should be reaching room temperature, so sit it in a large roasting tin and roast for 45 minutes. The chicken will be just cooked through and the skin will be a bit unappealing, but you'll be left with some delicious roasting juices that are the key to this dish. Remove the chicken from the roasting tin and preheat the barbecue for direct grilling (see page 11).

Once the barbecue is ready, grill the chicken for 10–15 minutes (the breasts and wings won't need quite as long as the thighs and legs). Keep turning the chicken until the skin is crispy and lightly charred. As soon as the chicken is ready, return it to the tray with those delicious roasting juices (which may have turned to jelly by this point). Quickly toss the chicken in the juices, season with the sea salt flakes and serve.

SEAFOOD PAELLA

Paella is traditionally cooked over a wood fire, giving it a delicious hint of smoke, and this recipe replicates that method. Unlike making a risotto, where stirring is essential, a paella should be left to cook gently without stirring. This stops too much starch being released from the rice, giving you tender individual grains rather than anything too creamy. A good stock is a must; the more flavoursome the broth, the better the finished paella.

SERVES 6 | PREP TIME: 25 MINUTES | COOK TIME: ABOUT 1 HOUR

FOR THE STOCK
olive oil, for frying
1 fennel bulb, finely sliced
12 large raw tiger prawns,
    shells on
1 litre good-quality chicken
    or fish stock
pinch of saffron threads

FOR THE PAELLA
olive oil, for frying
2 white onions, finely chopped
2 garlic cloves, crushed
4 ripe tomatoes, deseeded
    and diced
1 teaspoon hot smoked paprika
2 large squid, cleaned and
    sliced into rings
500g Bomba paella rice
12 large mussels, cleaned
    (ensure that they all close
    when tapped sharply on
    the work surface)
2 handfuls of clams,
    cleaned (ditto)
2 red peppers, roasted,
    peeled and deseeded,
    then torn into strips

TO SERVE
1 small bunch of flat-leaf
    parsley, leaves finely chopped
lemon wedges

You will need a large handful
of wood chips (see page 12),
soaked in warm water for
30 minutes.

First make the stock. Heat a little olive oil in a saucepan, add the fennel and fry for 5 minutes until softened. Peel and devein the prawns, then throw the shells and heads into the pan and fry for 5 minutes until they turn a deep pink colour. Pour over the stock, add the saffron and simmer gently for 20 minutes. Strain into a clean pan and keep warm.

Preheat the barbecue for direct grilling over a medium heat (see page 11) – anything too fierce will burn the bottom of the paella. Heat a good splash of oil in a large paella pan (about 46cm in diameter), add the onions and fry for 5 minutes until soft. Add the garlic, tomatoes and smoked paprika and fry for 5 minutes until the tomatoes start to break down. Add the squid and fry for a couple of minutes, then stir in the rice. Pour over the stock, give everything a quick stir and leave to simmer for 10 minutes.

Throw the drained, soaked wood chips onto the coals to start smoking gently. Arrange the prawns, mussels, clams and peppers over the top of the rice, close the lid and leave to cook gently. After about 10 minutes, check the seafood; if the mussels and clams have all opened and the prawns have all turned pink, the paella is ready (but throw out any odd shells that have failed to open). Remove it from the heat and leave to stand for 5 minutes before serving with the chopped parsley and lemon wedges.

GRILLED POLENTA
with ROSEMARY and TALEGGIO

These polenta cakes, stuffed with one of my favourite Italian cheeses, make a great meat-free main course or a pretty substantial side dish. Taste the mixture once you've added the Parmesan and adjust the seasoning before shaping into cakes, at which point it'll be too late. Once the cakes are on the grill they can be quite delicate, so only turn them when they're ready and do so carefully to keep them in one piece.

SERVES 4 | PREP TIME: 30 MINUTES PLUS CHILLING | COOK TIME: 45 MINUTES

600ml water
3 sprigs of rosemary,
    leaves finely chopped
½ teaspoon chilli flakes
½ teaspoon fine sea salt
150g quick-cook polenta
50g salted butter
75g Parmesan cheese,
    finely grated
olive oil, for greasing
    and brushing
80g Taleggio cheese,
    cut into 4 slices

**FOR THE AUBERGINE
AND TOMATO SAUCE**
1 medium aubergine,
    diced into 1cm chunks
olive oil, for frying
1 onion, finely chopped
2 garlic cloves, crushed
1 red chilli, finely chopped
400g can chopped tomatoes
1 small bunch of basil,
    leaves torn
sea salt and freshly ground
    black pepper

For the polenta, pour the water into a medium saucepan, add the rosemary, chilli flakes and salt and bring to the boil. Boil for 3 minutes, then pour in the polenta in a steady stream, whisking as you go. Cook for 2–3 minutes or according to the packet instructions, whisking constantly, until thickened. Remove from the heat, whisk in the butter and Parmesan and season to taste. Transfer the mixture to a bowl. Press a sheet of clingfilm onto the surface and leave to cool to room temperature. Don't let the polenta go completely cold, otherwise it'll be too firm to shape.

Lightly grease a 10cm round cookie cutter with a little olive oil and spoon one eighth of the mixture inside, pressing down with the back of a teaspoon. Lay a slice of Taleggio in the centre, then top with another eighth of the polenta. Press down to seal and then invert onto a lightly greased plate or baking tray. Continue with the remaining polenta and Taleggio until you have four cheese-stuffed rounds. Cover with clingfilm and chill for at least 30 minutes.

Meanwhile, make the sauce. Fry the aubergine in batches in a little olive oil in a sauté pan for 5 minutes until golden, then transfer to plate lined with kitchen paper to absorb any excess oil. Heat a little more oil and gently fry the onion for 5 minutes until soft. Add the garlic and chilli and fry for a couple of minutes, then stir in the tomatoes and aubergine. Bring to a simmer and cook for 15 minutes until thickened. Remove from the heat, stir in the basil and season to taste.

Preheat the barbecue for direct grilling (see page 11). Brush the polenta cakes on both sides with a little olive oil and grill for 10 minutes until golden and crisp, turning every few minutes. Serve with the spicy aubergine and tomato sauce.

BAKED CHEESE
with RATTE POTATOES

Baked cheese is nothing new but introducing smoke to the party lifts this classic to a whole new level. I use Tunworth, which has a rich, creamy centre that tastes faintly of fresh truffle and lends itself beautifully to baking. If you can't get hold of Tunworth, buy a good Camembert instead. I use Ratte potatoes, as they're long and slender and perfect for dipping in the cheese, but any small waxy potatoes will do. If you're feeding a crowd, you could bake several cheeses at once.

SERVES 4 AS A SNACK OR STARTER | **PREP TIME: 5 MINUTES** | **COOK TIME: 20 MINUTES**

250g Tunworth or Camembert cheese in a wooden box
1 sprig of rosemary, leaves finely chopped
1 garlic clove, peeled
pinch of sea salt flakes

TO SERVE
350g Ratte potatoes or other small waxy potatoes
fine sea salt
12 slices of cured ham

You will need a handful of wood chips (see page 12) – apple or cherry wood work best – soaked in warm water for 30 minutes.

Preheat the barbecue for indirect grilling (see page 11) and throw on the drained, soaked wood chips. Unwrap the cheese then lay it back in the box, ensuring that you remove any labels. Using a skewer or a small knife, make small holes in the top of the cheese, taking care not to penetrate too deeply; if you pierce the rind on the underside, all the good stuff will leak out during cooking.

Put the rosemary, garlic and salt into a mortar and grind to a fine paste with a pestle. Rub the paste into the surface of the cheese and then set it on the grill. Close the barbecue lid and cook for 20 minutes until the cheese is runny.

Meanwhile, boil the potatoes in a large pan of salted water for 8–10 minutes, then drain and leave to steam for a few minutes. When cool enough to handle, quarter them lengthways to make dipping wedges.

Serve the baked cheese with the potato wedges and cured ham.

HAND-HELD

CHILLI CHEESE BURGERS

The secret to a good beefburger is simplicity; great beef, simply seasoned and cooked well. I use a mixture of three different cuts: rump steak for richness, and short rib and brisket for texture and fat. The fat is crucial as it keeps it moist and makes a difference to the flavour. My butcher combines the three cuts and then coarsely minces them, passing the meat through the machine once so that the burger has defined texture. Be as gentle as possible when you shape the patties to avoid compressing the meat; you want the burger to fall apart as you eat it rather than being dense and chewy. Finally, just like a good steak, make sure you rest the burgers before serving them.

MAKES 8 | PREP TIME: 25 MINUTES PLUS CHILLING | COOK TIME: 15 MINUTES PLUS RESTING

FOR THE PATTIES
800g rump steak,
  coarsely minced
400g beef short rib meat,
  coarsely minced
400g brisket, coarsely minced
16g fine sea salt

FOR THE SAUCE
2 tablespoons tomato ketchup
2 tablespoons American
  mustard
2 tablespoons Mayonnaise
  (page 131)
2 gherkins, finely chopped

TO SERVE
8 slices of extra-mature
  Cheddar cheese
8 green chillies
8 Potato Buns (page 115)
  or brioche burger buns,
  split open
2 baby gem lettuces, leaves
  separated, washed and dried

You will need sixteen 15cm
squares of greaseproof paper.

Before you start, make sure the beef is well chilled; you'll need to work quickly to prevent the fat from melting in your hands. Season the beef evenly with the salt, gently combining everything with your hands. Divide the mixture into eight equal piles (to make sure they're all the same size, it's best to weigh them as you go; they should be 200g each). Gently shape the beef into balls and then press lightly into 1.5cm-thick rounds. Sandwich each burger between two squares of greaseproof paper, then chill for an hour.

Combine the sauce ingredients in a bowl and set aside.

Preheat the barbecue for direct grilling (see page 11) and remove the burgers from the fridge 15 minutes before cooking. Cook the burgers for 6–7 minutes, turning 2–3 times during cooking. After the last turn, top each burger with a slice of cheese and close the lid for a couple of minutes. Transfer the burgers to a wire rack to rest for 5 minutes.

While the burgers are resting, grill the chillies for 4–5 minutes until lightly charred and softened. Remove from the grill and finely slice. Toast the buns cut-side down on the grill for a minute until golden and lightly toasted.

To assemble, spread the bottom half of each roll with the sauce, top with a couple of lettuce leaves and lay a burger on top. Top with the chillies, then add the tops of the buns and press down lightly.

VARIATION: Swap the green chillies for a spoonful of Kimchi (page 124).

LAMB SHISH KEBABS
with PICKLED RED CABBAGE

This is a far cry from the grey cones of doner meat you see turning in dodgy kebab shop windows, affectionately known as an 'elephant's foot' in my student days. A proper Turkish shish kebab is an absolute pleasure; tender cubes of lamb in a rich marinade served up with crunchy pickled cabbage, soft flatbread, spicy chillies and plenty of hot sauce.

SERVES 4 │ **PREP TIME: 20 MINUTES PLUS CHILLING** │ **COOK TIME: 15 MINUTES PLUS RESTING**

1kg boneless leg of lamb,
  cut into 3cm cubes

FOR THE MARINADE
4 garlic cloves, crushed
2 tablespoons olive oil
finely grated zest and juice
  of 1 unwaxed lemon
1 tablespoon sweet
  smoked paprika
1 tablespoon ground cumin
2 teaspoons dried oregano
1 teaspoon sea salt

FOR THE PICKLED CABBAGE
½ small red cabbage,
  finely shredded
250ml white wine vinegar
75g caster sugar
2 teaspoons fine sea salt
2 teaspoons yellow
  mustard seeds
2 dried red chillies

TO SERVE
4 Flatbreads (page 117)
  or pitta breads
Pickled Green Chillies (page 126)
Tzatziki (page 122)
Hot Sauce (page 128)

You will need metal or wooden skewers; if you're using wooden ones, soak them in warm water for at least an hour.

Combine all the marinade ingredients in a large bowl, add the lamb and toss to coat. Cover with clingfilm and chill in the fridge for 2–3 hours or overnight.

Meanwhile, make the pickled cabbage. Put the cabbage into a large, heatproof bowl. Bring the vinegar, sugar, salt, mustard seeds and chillies to the boil in a small saucepan. Cook for 2 minutes, stirring occasionally, until the sugar has completely dissolved, then pour over the cabbage. Cover with clingfilm and leave to cool to room temperature. Stir occasionally as it's cooling, then transfer to the fridge and chill until needed. Drain before serving.

Remove the lamb from the fridge an hour before cooking and preheat the barbecue for direct grilling (see page 11). Thread the lamb onto skewers and grill for 10 minutes, turning regularly, until just cooked through. Transfer to a plate, cover with foil and leave to rest for 5 minutes. Serve with Flatbreads or pitta breads, Pickled Green Chillies, Tzatziki and Hot Sauce.

CHIPOTLE STEAK TACOS
with GUACAMOLE

This dish is designed for sharing as there's few things better than loading the table with a load of delicious food and some ice-cold beers and letting everyone get stuck in. Bavette comes from the flanks, meaning it's been worked hard and so is packed with flavour. It needs to be cooked hard and fast, served rare and sliced thinly across the grain. Do this and you'll have some seriously tasty, melt-in-the-mouth steak. If you prefer your steak more cooked, I'd opt for sirloin, which can handle longer cooking while staying tender. Track down the small corn tortillas from specialist Mexican food shops or online suppliers.

SERVES 4 | PREP TIME: 20 MINUTES PLUS CHILLING | COOK TIME: 15 MINUTES

4 bavette steaks, weighing
   150g each
2 tablespoons chipotle paste
1 teaspoon ground cumin
1 teaspoon cracked black pepper
½ teaspoon fine sea salt

FOR THE GUACAMOLE
1 red onion, finely chopped
2 green chillies, deseeded
   and finely chopped
1 garlic clove, crushed
2 unwaxed limes; finely
   grated zest of 1 and juice
   of both
2 ripe avocados
1 small bunch of coriander,
   finely chopped
sea salt and freshly ground
   black pepper

TO SERVE
16 small soft corn tortillas
Blackened Tomato Salsa
   (page 122)
100g feta, crumbled

Trim the steaks of any excess sinew and put them into a large bowl. Mix together the chipotle paste, cumin, pepper and salt, then rub into the steaks, ensuring that they're all evenly coated. Cover with clingfilm and chill in the fridge for an hour.

Remove the steaks from the fridge 30 minutes before cooking and preheat the barbecue for direct grilling (see page 11). To make the guacamole, combine the onion, chillies, garlic and lime zest and juice in a large bowl. Halve the avocados, remove the stones and scoop the flesh straight into the bowl; by preparing everything in this order, the avocado comes into contact with the lime juice as quickly as possible, keeping the guac fresh and vibrant green. Roughly mash with a fork, stir in the coriander and season to taste.

Grill the steaks for 5–6 minutes or until cooked to your liking, turning regularly. Set aside to rest for 5 minutes then thinly slice.

While the steaks are resting, wrap the tortillas in foil in parcels of four and lay on the grill to heat through. I wrap the tortillas in smaller parcels because it ensures that they heat evenly, and means you only have to unwrap one parcel at a time as you eat, keeping the others hot and fresh through the meal.

To serve, spoon a little guacamole onto a tortilla and top with a few slices of steak. Top with more guacamole, some salsa and crumbled feta.

VARIATION: For a veggie version, swap the steaks for four large portobello mushrooms and marinate and cook as above; just wrap the mushrooms in foil once they come off the grill to keep them moist.

CHEESE and BACON DOGS

This cheese sauce is ridiculously addictive, so if there should be any left over, make sure you have some tortilla chips to hand. It will thicken as it cools, so if you make it in advance, press a sheet of clingfilm onto the surface to stop a skin forming and then add a little extra milk as you reheat it. I always buy ready-made crispy onions for these dogs, as they're one of my guilty pleasures (and frankly a bit of a pain to make at home).

MAKES 8 | PREP TIME: 15 MINUTES | COOK TIME: 35 MINUTES

8 rashers of smoked
  streaky bacon

FOR THE CHEESE SAUCE
20g plain flour
20g salted butter
½ teaspoon cayenne pepper
350ml hot whole milk
200g extra-mature Cheddar
  cheese, grated
75g drained, pickled green
  jalapeños, finely chopped
2 tablespoons jalapeño brine

FOR THE DOGS
8 fat Frankfurter sausages
8 Potato Rolls (page 115),
  split open
American mustard
ready-made crispy onions

Preheat the oven to 180°C/gas mark 4. Line a baking tray with greaseproof paper and lay out the bacon rashers in a single layer. Top with a second sheet of paper and lay another baking tray on top. Cook for 15 minutes until crispy, then set aside to cool. Crumble the bacon into small pieces and set aside.

Preheat the barbecue for direct grilling (see page 11). To make the cheese sauce, cook the flour, butter and cayenne pepper in a saucepan over a medium heat for 2–3 minutes, stirring until the mixture starts to smell nutty. Remove from the heat and whisk in one-third of the hot milk. Return to the heat and gradually whisk in the remaining milk until you have a smooth sauce. Cook gently for 5 minutes until thickened slightly, whisking constantly. Stir in the cheese until smooth, then stir in the jalapeños and brine. Cover with a lid and leave next to the barbecue to keep warm.

Grill the sausages for 6–8 minutes, turning regularly. Move them to one side of the grill, then toast the cut side of the rolls.

To assemble, spread the insides of each roll with mustard and lay a sausage on top. Spoon over some cheese sauce and finish with the bacon and crispy onions.

CHILLI DOGS

Far from being something to bulk out your barbecue, hot dogs can be loaded up with delicious toppings to make them the star of the show, and let's face it; they're a good excuse to get messy. I always use Chicago-style jumbo frankfurters rather than a standard pork sausage that you'd get from the butcher; for me, a proper dog is all about that slightly squeaky exterior and dense, smoky filling. Hot dogs hardly need any cooking – just a quick flash over the coals to heat them through – so you can put a bit of time and effort into making these awesome toppings.

MAKES 8 | PREP TIME: 15 MINUTES | COOK TIME: 2 HOURS 40 MINUTES

FOR THE CHILLI
olive oil, for frying
120g chorizo, finely diced
400g coarsely minced beef
2 onions, finely chopped
2 garlic cloves, crushed
1 teaspoon ground cumin
1 teaspoon ground cinnamon
1 teaspoon chilli flakes
2 tablespoons tomato purée
400g can chopped tomatoes
500ml hot beef stock or
　chicken stock
1 dried ancho chilli
400g can kidney beans,
　drained
sea salt and freshly ground
　black pepper

FOR THE DOGS
8 fat frankfurter sausages
8 Potato Rolls (page 115),
　split open
American mustard
2 sweet white onions,
　finely chopped
1 bunch of coriander,
　finely chopped

Heat a little oil in a heavy-based casserole, add the chorizo and fry gently for 5 minutes until crisp. Set a sieve over a bowl and tip the chorizo in; you'll end up with some chorizo oil in the bowl.

Pour half the collected oil back into the pan, crank the heat up and add the beef. Fry for 5 minutes until golden brown and starting to turn crisp, then tip into the sieve with the chorizo.

Return the remaining oil to the pan, add the onions and fry for 10 minutes until soft and caramelised. Add the garlic and spices and cook for a further 2 minutes. Add the tomato purée and fry for 2–3 minutes, then pour in the chopped tomatoes and hot stock and bring to a simmer. Return the chorizo and beef to the pan, drop in the ancho chilli and simmer gently for 1½ hours, stirring occasionally. Add the beans and cook for a further 30 minutes. Remove from the heat and adjust the seasoning.

Preheat the barbecue for direct grilling (see page 11). Grill the sausages for 6–8 minutes until warmed through and lightly charred, turning regularly. Move them to one side of the grill and then lightly toast the cut side of the rolls.

To assemble, spread the insides of each roll with mustard and lay a sausage on top. Spoon over some of the chilli and finish with plenty of onions and coriander.

BOURBON-GLAZED BABY BACK RIBS

Meat cooked on the bone always tastes better, and ribs pretty much top the charts in that regard. There are two main types of ribs: spare ribs and baby back. Without delving too far into porcine anatomy, spare ribs are the big chunky ones from the belly whereas, coming from the loin, baby back are smaller, leaner and more tender. I prefer baby back as they involve more gnawing and the meat always tastes a little sweeter. I use the same dry rub as the Pulled Pork recipe (page 142) and finish it with a sweet, sharp glaze laced with bourbon. Do try this with a rack of spare ribs, but they'll need a couple more hours cooking.

MAKES 2 FULL RACKS/SERVES 4 | PREP TIME: 5 MINUTES | COOK TIME: 4½ HOURS PLUS RESTING

2 full racks of baby back ribs
100ml apple juice
100ml cider vinegar

FOR THE DRY RUB
2 tablespoons cracked
   black pepper
1 tablespoon fine sea salt
1 tablespoon demerara sugar
1 tablespoon paprika

FOR THE GLAZE
100ml Quick Sharp Barbecue
   Sauce (page 128) or other
   sharp barbecue sauce
75ml bourbon

Remove the ribs from the fridge 30 minutes before cooking and preheat the barbecue for indirect grilling (see page 11). Grind the rub ingredients to a fine powder using a pestle and mortar. Put the ribs into a large roasting tray and coat evenly in the rub. Lay the ribs meat-side up on the grill, close the lid and cook for an hour. Combine the apple juice and vinegar in a spray bottle and spray on both sides, then cook for a further hour.

Lay each rack of ribs on a large sheet of foil, give them another good spray with the vinegar mixture then wrap in the foil and return to the grill for a further 2 hours.

Change the barbecue set-up to direct grilling (see page 11). Combine the barbecue sauce and bourbon in a small saucepan and set on the grill.

Unwrap the ribs, lay on the grill meat-side up and cook for 15 minutes, turning and basting with the glaze; you'll need to be careful as you turn the ribs because they'll be really tender by this point, with the meat falling off the bone. Transfer to a board and leave to rest for 10 minutes, then serve.

STICKY LAMB RIBS

Lamb ribs are a fairly unusual cut, but lend themselves to smoking and grilling. They're seriously big on flavour, with a decent amount of fat, so stay beautifully moist. You'll need to ask your butcher for breast of lamb on the bone with the fatty tip removed. Also ask for the chine bone to be cut away, otherwise you won't be able to cut the rack into individual ribs.

SERVES 4 | PREP TIME: 5 MINUTES | COOK TIME: 3¼ HOURS PLUS RESTING

2 breasts of lamb on the bone, weighing approx. 700g each (trimmed weight)
1 tablespoon fine sea salt
1 tablespoon coarsely ground black pepper

FOR THE GLAZE
2 tablespoons tamarind water (see note)
2 tablespoons fish sauce
2 tablespoons palm sugar
2 tablespoons sriracha chilli sauce

TO SERVE
1 tablespoon toasted sesame seeds
lime wedges

Preheat the barbecue or smoker for indirect grilling (see page 11). Season the lamb with the salt and pepper then lay on the grill, close the lid and smoke for 3 hours, turning halfway through. Remove from the barbecue or smoker and leave to cool.

Change the barbecue set-up to direct grilling (see page 11). Combine the glaze ingredients in a small bowl and stir until the palm sugar has completely dissolved. Lay the lamb ribs on the grill and cook for 15 minutes, turning regularly and basting with the glaze. Remove the ribs from the grill, give a final brush with the glaze and set aside to rest for 5 minutes.

Slice the lamb into individual ribs, scatter with the toasted sesame seeds and serve with lime wedges.

NOTE: You can buy tamarind liquid in a jar or a bottle, but it's often laden with preservatives or heavily sweetened, which defeats the object, as tamarind provides the sour element of the glaze. To make tamarind water, buy a block of tamarind pulp, tear off an egg-sized chunk and pour over enough boiling water to barely cover. Leave to soak for 15 minutes, then pass through a sieve to remove any seeds and fibres and it's ready to use.

PORK BANH MI

Few sandwiches are better than this Vietnamese street food snack. It's got everything
you need: smoky, lemongrass-scented pork, crunchy pickled vegetables, fresh herbs
and a wicked sesame aioli. It's not strictly traditional as I've left out the pâté, but it's
vibrant, fresh and utterly delicious.

MAKES 4 | PREP TIME: 30 MINUTES PLUS CHILLING | COOK TIME: 15 MINUTES

500g pork neck fillet

FOR THE MARINADE
4 garlic cloves, peeled
2 lemongrass stalks, tough
   outer leaves discarded,
   finely chopped
2 spring onions, roughly
   chopped
1 red chilli, roughly chopped
2 tablespoons fish sauce
1 tablespoon dark soy sauce
2 teaspoons light brown
   soft sugar

FOR THE SESAME AIOLI
1 medium egg yolk
1 small garlic clove, crushed
100ml vegetable oil
1 tablespoon toasted sesame oil
1½ teaspoons rice vinegar
½ teaspoon fish sauce

**FOR THE PICKLED
   VEGETABLES**
1 large daikon
2 large carrots
2 tablespoons caster sugar
2 teaspoons sea salt flakes
2 tablespoons rice vinegar

TO SERVE
4 small baguettes
2 spring onions, shredded
1 bunch of coriander,
   leaves picked
1 bunch of mint, leaves picked

Cut the pork into 2cm slices and put into large bowl. Combine
the marinade ingredients in a liquidiser and blend until smooth.
Pour over the pork and toss to coat, then cover with clingfilm
and chill for at least 2 hours; overnight is even better.

Meanwhile, make the aioli. Put the egg yolk and garlic into
a large bowl and whisk together until smooth. Combine the
oils in a jug and, whisking constantly, begin to pour into the bowl
in a very thin, steady stream. Continue steadily adding the oil and
whisking until it's all incorporated. Whisk in the vinegar and fish
sauce, then set aside.

For the pickled vegetables, peel the daikon and carrots and cut
into thin matchsticks. Put the vegetables into a large bowl with
the sugar and salt, then gently work everything together with
your hands. Keep tumbling and gently kneading the vegetables
for 5 minutes until they've softened. Drain off the excess liquid,
stir in the vinegar and set aside.

Remove the pork from the fridge 30 minutes before cooking
and preheat the barbecue for direct grilling (see page 11). Grill
the pork for 10 minutes until cooked through and lightly charred,
then remove from the grill and leave to rest for a few minutes.

Split the baguettes lengthways and lightly toast the insides
on the grill. Spread with the aioli and top with the pickled
vegetables. Thinly slice the pork, pile into the baguettes
and top with the spring onions and herbs.

'NDUJA PIZZA

If you own a barbecue, you also own a pretty decent pizza oven. By using a pizza stone, or even a heavy baking tray, you can cook beautifully light, crisp pizzas in minutes. The basic dough and sauce can be used for any pizza, so play around with toppings. The biggest mistake people make is to add too many ingredients, which means the crust is cooked well before the toppings have got going. Use your toppings sparingly, spread in an even layer, and you can't go wrong. This recipe uses one of my favourite ingredients, 'nduja. It's a fiery Italian salami from Calabria with a soft, spreadable consistency, perfect to dab over a pizza.

MAKES 4 | PREP TIME: 30 MINUTES PLUS RISING TIME | COOK TIME: ABOUT 5 MINUTES

FOR THE DOUGH
400g strong white bread flour
100g fine semolina, plus extra
    for dusting
7g sachet fast-action
    dried yeast
1½ teaspoons fine sea salt
1 tablespoon honey
330ml lager
olive oil, for greasing

FOR THE SAUCE
2 tablespoons extra virgin
    olive oil
2 garlic cloves, crushed
pinch of chilli flakes
600g good-quality Italian
    canned chopped tomatoes
pinch of caster sugar
pinch of fine sea salt

TOPPINGS
400g buffalo mozzarella
100g 'nduja
50g Parmesan cheese,
    grated
1 small bunch of basil,
    leaves torn

To make the dough, combine the dry ingredients and honey in the bowl of a stand mixer fitted with a dough hook. Start the machine on a low speed and pour in the lager. Knead on a low speed for 3 minutes, then increase the speed to the next setting and knead for a further 6 minutes. If you're making the dough by hand, combine the ingredients in a large mixing bowl to form a rough dough. Tip out onto a work surface and knead for 10 minutes.

Transfer the dough to a large bowl, lightly greased with olive oil, and cover with a clean tea towel. Leave somewhere warm for an hour or until the dough has doubled in size. Fire up the barbecue to a high temperature for direct grilling (see page 11).

Meanwhile, make the sauce. Heat the oil in a saucepan over a very low heat, add the garlic and chilli flakes and cook gently for 2 minutes. Add the tomatoes, sugar and salt and bring to a gentle simmer. Cook for 10 minutes, then remove from the heat and leave to cool.

Set a pizza stone or heavy baking tray on the grill, close the lid and open the vents as wide as possible. Dust the work surface with semolina, turn the dough out and divide into four equal balls. Roll each out thinly to make a large round, then spread with the cooled tomato sauce. Tear the mozzarella into small pieces and dot over the sauce. Dot the 'nduja over the top and finish with a scattering of Parmesan.

Use a pizza peel or thin, flat baking tray to lift the pizzas from the work surface and slide them onto the hot pizza stone or heavy baking tray. Close the lid and bake for 3–4 minutes (depending on how hot you can make your barbecue) until the base is crisp and the cheese is golden and bubbling. As soon as each pizza is ready, scatter over a few torn basil leaves, cut into slices and dive in.

ONION BURGERS

Veggie burgers make me a bit sad. They are often brought to a barbecue still frozen, thin and grey. By the time they're cooked, they have either turned cardboard dry or have melted and started to fall through the grill. So I came up with this – a thick slab of onion, marinated in garlic and thyme, then grilled slowly until soft and caramelised. It eats like a burger, has a sweet, smoky flavour and kicks those tasteless hockey pucks into touch.

MAKES 4 | PREP TIME: 15 MINUTES PLUS MARINATING | COOK TIME: 20 MINUTES

2 very large onions, peeled
4 sprigs of thyme,
    leaves picked
1 garlic clove, peeled
pinch of sea salt flakes
olive oil, for marinating
    and frying
1 tablespoon sherry vinegar
1 teaspoon dark brown
    soft sugar

TO SERVE
3 tablespoons Mayonnaise
    (page 131)
1 teaspoon coarsely ground
    black pepper
4 slices of extra-mature
    Cheddar cheese
4 Potato Buns (page 115)
    or brioche burger buns
2 red peppers, roasted,
    halved and deseeded
1 baby gem lettuce, leaves
    separated, washed and dried

You will need 12 thin
wooden skewers, soaked
in warm water for at least
an hour.

Remove the tops and roots from each onion, then slice two 1.5cm-thick rounds from the middle of each. Finely slice the leftover bits of onion and set aside. Put the thyme leaves and garlic into a mortar, add the salt and grind to a fine paste, then stir in 1 tablespoon of olive oil. Brush over the onion steaks in a dish, cover with clingfilm and chill for a couple of hours to allow the flavours to mingle.

Meanwhile, heat a little olive oil in a heavy-based frying pan, add the sliced leftover onion and fry very gently for 20 minutes until soft and caramelised. Don't add any salt to the pan; it will draw the moisture out of the onions and prevent them from caramelising. Add the vinegar and sugar, increase the heat and cook for a further 5 minutes until dark and sticky. Remove from the heat and set aside.

Preheat the barbecue for direct grilling (see page 11). Combine the Mayonnaise and black pepper in a small bowl. Thread the onion steaks onto the drained, soaked skewers; I use three per slice of onion, inserted at evenly spaced intervals through the side and passing right through the middle of the onion steak to hold all the rings together. Grill the onion steaks for 10–12 minutes until lightly charred and softened, turning regularly. Move to a cooler part of the grill, lay a slice of cheese on each and close the lid for a couple of minutes until the cheese has melted.

Toast the cut sides of the buns and then spread the bases with the black pepper mayonnaise. Top each with half a roasted red pepper and lay an onion steak on top, then add a spoonful of the caramelised onions, a lettuce leaf and the bun tops.

VARIATION: For a spicy version, add ½ teaspoon of chilli flakes to the caramelised onions at the start of cooking.

PORK SOUVLAKI

These fragrant pork kebabs with their sharp, herby marinade instantly transport me back to Greece. I make them as they're served in tavernas and street food stalls: tightly wrapped in a warm flatbread with garlicky tzatziki, fresh tomatoes, finely sliced onions and, if you don't mind a bit of a carb fest, a handful of chips.

SERVES 4 | PREP TIME: 15 MINUTES PLUS CHILLING | COOK TIME: 15 MINUTES PLUS RESTING

1kg pork shoulder, trimmed
    of all excess fat and sinew,
    cut into 3cm cubes
4 large green chillies

FOR THE MARINADE
finely grated zest and juice
    of 1 unwaxed lemon
3 garlic cloves, crushed
2 tablespoons finely chopped
    fresh oregano
2 tablespoons olive oil
1 tablespoon red wine vinegar
2 teaspoons dried mint
1 teaspoon ground cumin
1 teaspoon chilli flakes
1 teaspoon fine sea salt

TO SERVE
Flatbreads (page 117)
Tzatziki (page 122)
2 ripe tomatoes, finely sliced
2 red onions, finely sliced
chips (optional)

You will need metal or wooden
skewers; if you're using wooden
skewers, soak them in warm
water for at least an hour.

Combine the marinade ingredients in a large bowl, add the pork and toss to coat. Cover with clingfilm and chill in the fridge for 2–3 hours or overnight.

Remove the pork from the fridge 30 minutes before cooking and preheat the barbecue for direct grilling (see page 11). Thread the pork onto skewers and grill for 10–12 minutes until cooked through, turning regularly. Grill the chillies alongside the pork until softened and lightly blistered, turning regularly too. Remove the pork and chillies from the grill, leaving the pork to rest for 5 minutes.

To serve, spread a Flatbread with Tzatziki, pile the pork on top and add a grilled chilli, sliced tomatoes, red onion and chips, if you like. Wrap tightly and serve.

VARIATION: This also works well with chicken – substitute the pork with the same quantity of skinless thigh fillets.

GREEN CHICKEN KEBABS

These delicious kebabs came about by accident when I had to bulk out a meal for some unexpected guests and all I had was a few chicken breasts, so I quickly threw together a marinade with what was to hand. They were so popular that they've become a regular favourite. By using lemon juice and loads of fresh herbs, and allowing plenty of marinating time, the chicken takes on a deep green colour and stays really succulent.

SERVES 4 | PREP TIME: 15 MINUTES PLUS CHILLING | COOK TIME: 10 MINUTES, PLUS RESTING

finely grated zest of 2 unwaxed
    lemons and juice of 1
75ml olive oil
4 garlic cloves, peeled
50g bunch of basil
50g bunch of flat-leaf parsley
25g bunch of coriander
½ teaspoon fine sea salt
4 free-range skinless,
    boneless chicken breasts,
    cut into 3cm cubes

You will need metal or
wooden skewers; if you're
using wooden skewers,
soak them in warm water
for at least an hour.

Combine all the ingredients, except the chicken, in a liquidiser and blend until smooth. Put the chicken into a large bowl, pour the marinade over and toss to coat. Don't season at this stage; the salt will draw the moisture from the chicken and make it tough. Cover with clingfilm and chill for 4 hours or overnight if possible.

Remove the chicken from the fridge an hour before cooking and preheat the barbecue for direct grilling (see page 11). Thread the chicken onto skewers and grill for 10 minutes until cooked through, turning occasionally. Transfer to a warm plate to rest for 5 minutes before serving.

CHICKEN SATAY

When it comes to satay, I have to insist that it's done properly. A recipe that involves peanut butter is definitely not satay. Proper satay, the stuff grilled over low charcoal barbecues on Malaysian and Indonesian streets, is the incredible combination of fragrant skewers of lightly charred, marinated meat and a rich, sweet roasted peanut sauce. The same ingredients crop up in both the marinade and the sauce, which are pretty quick and easy to prepare if you own a food processor.

SERVES 4 | PREP TIME: 30 MINUTES PLUS CHILLING | COOK TIME: ABOUT 30 MINUTES

500g free-range skinless chicken thigh fillets, cut into small bite-sized pieces

FOR THE MARINADE
2 tablespoons vegetable oil
4 shallots, roughly chopped
3 lemongrass stalks, tough outer leaves discarded, roughly chopped
4 garlic cloves, peeled
2 red chillies, roughly chopped
thumb-sized piece of fresh galangal, peeled and roughly chopped
thumb-sized piece of fresh turmeric, peeled and roughly chopped (or 1½ teaspoons ground turmeric)
2 tablespoons ketjap manis (Indonesian sweet soy sauce)
2 teaspoons ground coriander
1 teaspoon ground cumin

FOR THE SAUCE
4 dried red chillies
75g tamarind pulp
100g unsalted roasted peanuts
2 shallots, roughly chopped
thumb-sized piece of fresh galangal, peeled and roughly chopped
3 garlic cloves, peeled
1 lemongrass stalk, tough outer leaves discarded, roughly chopped
1½ tablespoons vegetable oil
2 teaspoons palm sugar
2 teaspoons ketjap manis

lime wedges, to serve

You will need metal or wooden skewers; if you're using wooden ones, soak them in warm water for at least an hour.

Put the marinade ingredients into a food processor and blend to a smooth paste. Pour over the chicken in a bowl and stir to coat. Cover with clingfilm and chill for at least 6 hours or overnight if possible.

Meanwhile, make the sauce. Put the chillies and tamarind into separate bowls, pour over enough boiling water to cover and leave to stand. Preheat the oven to 200°C/gas mark 6. Spread out the peanuts on a baking tray and roast for 10 minutes, shaking the tray halfway through. Set aside to cool, then crush with a pestle and mortar.

Put the shallots, galangal, garlic, lemongrass and vegetable oil into a food processor. Drain the chillies, discard any stalks and add to the food processor, then blend to a smooth paste. Heat a wok or large frying pan over a medium heat, add the paste and cook for 3–4 minutes until the oil begins to separate from the other ingredients. Pour the tamarind water through a sieve into the pan, add the palm sugar and ketjap manis and cook for 2–3 minutes. Remove the pan from the heat and stir in the crushed peanuts. Set aside to cool.

Remove the chicken from the fridge 30 minutes before cooking and preheat the barbecue for direct grilling (see page 11). Thread the chicken onto skewers and grill for 8–10 minutes until cooked through and lightly charred, turning regularly.

Serve the chicken skewers with the sauce and lime wedges.

CHICKEN WINGS with HOT SAUCE and BLUE CHEESE

Traditionally chicken wings are deep-fried from raw until crisp and then tossed in a vinegary hot sauce finished with butter. This achieves the essential crisp skin, but deep-frying for such a long time can turn the chicken a bit dry. After extensive research, I found that some of the best places in New York confit or slow roast their wings first, then finish them in the fryer. So I experimented with smoking the wings to keep them really tender, then finishing them over direct heat. They were good, but there was no way of getting that all-over crispy skin, the hallmark of a great wing. Back to the fryer it was then. The result was the perfect wing; soft and smoky on the inside, with crisp skin slathered in hot sauce.

SERVES 6 | PREP TIME: 10 MINUTES | COOK TIME: 1¼ HOURS

1.5kg free-range chicken wings
2 teaspoons fine sea salt
150ml Hot Sauce (page 128)
25g cold salted butter, cubed
vegetable oil, for deep-frying

FOR THE BLUE CHEESE DIP
150g Roquefort cheese, crumbled
150ml soured cream

TO SERVE
3 celery sticks, cut into matchsticks
2 large carrots, peeled and cut into matchsticks

You will need a handful of wood chips (see page 12), soaked in warm water for 30 minutes.

Preheat the barbecue for indirect grilling (see page 11) and throw on the drained wood chips. Season the chicken with the salt and arrange on the grill in an even layer. Close the lid and cook for 1 hour, then remove from the grill and leave to cool slightly.

While the wings are smoking, make the blue cheese dip. Combine 100g of the Roquefort and the soured cream in a small food processor and blend until smooth. Tip into a bowl and stir in the remaining cheese. Cover with clingfilm and chill until you're ready to serve.

Pour the Hot Sauce into a saucepan, bring to a gentle simmer and whisk in the butter. Pour into a large bowl and set aside while you fry the wings.

Heat the oil in a deep fryer or deep-sided, heavy-based saucepan to 180°C and line a baking tray with kitchen paper. Fry the wings, in batches, for 3–4 minutes and then remove from the oil and drain on kitchen paper. Immediately toss the wings in the Hot Sauce mixture and serve with the blue cheese dip and token vegetables.

PAN CON TOMATE

These little snacks rely heavily on great ingredients. The tomatoes should be perfectly ripe and sweet; the garlic fresh, firm and fiery. The bread needs to be robust enough to withstand grilling and dense enough to hold all the juices, while the salt must be flaky for that lovely crunch. The oil needs to be the best you can get; rich, dark and peppery enough to make your tongue tingle. This is the perfect snack to make when your guests arrive: delicious, easy and fast to prepare, it will wake up everyone's palates ahead of the main event.

MAKES 18 PIECES | PREP TIME: 5 MINUTES | COOK TIME: 2–3 MINUTES

2 ripe tomatoes, the
   best you can find
6 large slices of good-quality
   white bread, such as
   sourdough or similar
3 fat garlic cloves, peeled
sea salt
extra virgin olive oil,
   for drizzling

Preheat the barbecue for direct grilling (see page 11).

Quarter the tomatoes, remove the tough cores and then roughly chop. Put into a small food processor and pulse until you have a chunky pulp.

Lay the bread on the grill and toast for 2–3 minutes until golden brown and lightly charred, turning occasionally. Immediately rub with the peeled garlic; the toasted surface of the bread will act as an abrasive and grate the garlic.

Arrange the toasted bread on a serving platter and spoon over the tomatoes. Season with plenty of sea salt and then drizzle with olive oil. Devour and let the juice run down your chin.

FROM
THE
SEA

GALICIAN OCTOPUS

This is a version of one of my favourite tapas dishes, which I've adapted slightly for the barbecue. I'd never usually advocate the use of frozen fish or seafood over fresh, but there is an exception to every rule. When octopus is frozen, the ice crystals permeate and tenderise the meat, meaning it'll be beautifully soft when you come to grill it.

SERVES 4 | PREP TIME: 20 MINUTES PLUS COOLING AND CHILLING | COOK TIME: 1 HOUR

2kg frozen octopus
  tentacles, defrosted
fine sea salt
2 large waxy potatoes
2 tablespoons olive oil
1 garlic clove, crushed
juice of ½ lemon,
  plus wedges to serve
1 teaspoon sweet smoked
  paprika
1 small bunch of flat-leaf
  parsley, finely chopped

Bring a large pan of water to the boil, add the octopus and return to the boil. Reduce the heat slightly and simmer gently for 45 minutes. Drain and leave to cool, then transfer to the fridge and chill for at least an hour.

Preheat the barbecue for direct grilling (see page 11) and bring a large pan of salted water to the boil. Peel the potatoes, cut into 5mm-thick slices and add to the pan, then simmer for 12–15 minutes until tender. Drain thoroughly.

Meanwhile, toss the octopus in the olive oil and garlic and season with salt. Grill for 10 minutes until lightly charred and warmed through, turning regularly.

Remove the octopus from the grill to a chopping board and cut into thick slices. Toss in the lemon juice, paprika and parsley, then add the potatoes and toss together gently, taking care not to break up the potatoes. Transfer to a warm plate and serve with lemon wedges.

BAJAN BLACKENED FISH KEBABS

Some of the best fish I've ever eaten was in Barbados where I kept seeing 'blackened' fish on menus and assumed it meant that it had been barbecued. After chatting to a local chef I discovered the name comes from the spice mixture used in the dry rub. A few crucial things: use a firm-fleshed fish, go heavy on the black pepper and always serve with a fiery pepper sauce.

SERVES 4 | PREP TIME: 10 MINUTES PLUS MARINATING | COOK TIME: 10 MINUTES

500g firm cod or haddock loin, cut into 4cm chunks

FOR THE BLACKENING SEASONING
1 teaspoon black peppercorns
1 teaspoon dried thyme
1 teaspoon paprika
1 teaspoon garlic powder
½ teaspoon fine sea salt

FOR THE PEPPER SAUCE
4 green Scotch Bonnet chillies
½ sweet white onion, finely chopped
½ garlic clove, crushed
½ teaspoon fine sea salt
pinch of caster sugar
1 tablespoon white wine vinegar

lime wedges, to serve

You will need metal or wooden skewers; if you're using wooden skewers, soak them in warm water for at least an hour.

Preheat the barbecue for direct grilling (see page 11). Put the spices for the seasoning into a mortar and grind to a fine powder with a pestle. Tip the spice mix onto a large plate or baking tray, add the fish pieces and toss to coat. Thread the fish onto skewers and set aside for 15 minutes.

To make the pepper sauce, roughly chop the chillies (you can deseed them if you want a milder sauce) and put into a small food processor with the onion, garlic, salt and sugar, then blend to a smooth paste. Add the vinegar and pulse briefly to incorporate. Pour into a small serving bowl and set aside.

Grill the fish kebabs for 10 minutes, turning regularly. Serve with the pepper sauce and lime wedges.

PRAWNS and SCALLOPS
with CHILLI and LIME

Barbecuing prawns and scallops works so well; the smoky flavour from the coals and the sweet, succulent seafood are the perfect match. The trick with the prawns is to peel away the middle section of the shells while leaving the rest intact, which makes them easy to eat without missing out on the delicious heads. Ensure that your barbecue is as hot as possible so that you achieve a good char on the shellfish without overcooking them.

SERVES 4 | PREP TIME: 15 MINUTES PLUS MARINATING | COOK TIME: 6–7 MINUTES

finely grated zest of
  2 unwaxed limes
2 red bird's eye chillies,
  finely chopped
2 garlic cloves, crushed
2 tablespoons fish sauce
2 tablespoons olive oil
12 large raw tiger prawns,
  shell on
12 large scallops, shelled
  and cleaned (see page 73)
25g unsalted butter, melted
lime wedges, to serve

You will need metal or wooden skewers; if you're using wooden skewers, soak them in warm water for at least an hour.

Combine the lime zest, chillies, garlic, fish sauce and olive oil in a large bowl and whisk to combine. Peel the middle sections of the shells from the prawns, leaving the heads and tails intact, and devein. Add the prawns and scallops to the marinade and toss to coat. Cover the bowl with clingfilm and leave to marinate in the fridge for 30 minutes.

Preheat the barbecue for direct grilling (see page 11). Thread the prawns and scallops onto skewers and grill for 6–7 minutes, turning and brushing with the melted butter regularly. Serve with lime wedges.

MONKFISH in BANANA LEAVES

Cooking in banana leaves imparts a unique flavour; a sort of herby, smoked tea. If you can't find them, wrap the fish in a single layer of greaseproof paper and then in foil. Monkfish is meaty, sweet and robust enough to stand up to the spicy marinade, but any firm-fleshed white fish or even some fat, juicy prawns will work. I use a combination of chillies; larger, milder ones for colour and sweetness, fresh bird's eye for a fiery kick and dried chillies for a smoky background heat.

SERVES 4 | PREP TIME: 15 MINUTES PLUS MARINATING | COOK TIME: 10 MINUTES

600g monkfish fillet, cut
   into bite-sized pieces
2 banana leaves, washed

FOR THE MARINADE
2 lemongrass stalks,
   tough outer leaves
   discarded, chopped
thumb-sized piece of fresh
   galangal, peeled and
   finely chopped
3cm piece of fresh turmeric,
   peeled and chopped or
   ½ teaspoon ground
   turmeric
3 large red chillies, chopped
3 red bird's eye chillies,
   chopped
5 garlic cloves, crushed
6 Thai shallots, peeled
   and chopped
6 dried red Thai chillies,
   deseeded
4 kaffir lime leaves,
   finely chopped
1 tablespoon fish sauce

Thai sticky rice, to serve

You will need 8 wooden
cocktail sticks or small
wooden skewers, soaked
in warm water for at
least an hour.

Combine all the marinade ingredients in a food processor and blend until smooth. Pour into a large bowl, add the monkfish and toss to coat. Cover the bowl with clingfilm and leave to marinate in the fridge for a couple of hours.

Preheat the barbecue for direct grilling (see page 11). Cut the banana leaves in half lengthways and slice away the thick central stem. Trim the rounded ends of the leaves to leave four large rectangular sheets. Spoon a quarter of the fish onto the end of each sheet and roll up, tucking in the sides to make a neat parcel. Secure each parcel with a couple of soaked cocktail sticks or small skewers. Lay the parcels on the grill and cook for 10 minutes, turning halfway through cooking, then set aside to rest for a couple of minutes. Unwrap and serve with Thai sticky rice.

COAL-ROAST SCALLOPS with SWEETCORN and SERRANO HAM

This recipe shows that barbecues aren't all about big lumps of meat and can be used to cook some really refined dishes. It makes a great starter, and if you get the prep done in advance, it's ready in no time.

SERVES 4 | PREP TIME: 20 MINUTES | COOK TIME: ABOUT 20 MINUTES

12 medium scallops
    in their shells
olive oil, for coating
sea salt
sweet smoked paprika,
    for seasoning

FOR THE SWEETCORN PURÉE
2 sweetcorn cobs
fine sea salt
1 garlic clove, peeled
75ml double cream
freshly ground black pepper

4 slices of Serrano ham,
    to serve

Preheat the oven to 180°C/gas mark 4. Preheat the barbecue and remove the grill. Open the scallop shells and carefully remove the flesh using the side of a dessertspoon. Peel away the frills and the muscle that attaches the scallop to the shell. You can leave the roe on or off; I like the taste but don't think they add anything to this dish. Rinse the rounded halves of the shells and pat dry; you can get rid of the flat halves.

For the sweetcorn purée, shave the sweetcorn kernels from the cobs with a sharp knife and drop into a pan of salted boiling water along with the garlic clove. Cook for 5 minutes and then drain, reserving the cooking water. Tip the corn and garlic into a liquidiser with the cream and blend for a couple of minutes until smooth. Pass through a sieve into a clean pan. Season to taste with salt and pepper and set aside.

Lay the ham between two sheets of greaseproof paper and sandwich between two flat baking trays. Bake for 10 minutes until crisp, then set aside to cool.

Toss the scallops in a little olive oil and season with salt and smoked paprika. Push the scallop shells into the coals (depending on the size of your barbecue, you may need to do this in a couple of batches) and leave to heat up for a couple of minutes. Lay the scallops in the shells and cook for 1 minute on each side. Remove the scallops from the shells with tongs and leave to rest on a warm plate for a minute while you retrieve the shells.

To serve, spoon a little sweetcorn purée into each shell, top with a scallop and break over the crispy ham. Finish with a pinch more smoked paprika.

TIP: To stop the shells sliding around on the plate when you serve, put a small mound of rock salt underneath each one.

TUNA NIÇOISE
AS IT SHOULD BE

This is a great salad if you're looking to impress. The blanching and refreshing, which keeps everything fresh and vibrant, means that you can do most of the work in advance. If I'm cooking for a large group, I'll prep the eggs, beans, tomatoes and dressing hours ahead. However, I have to insist that the potatoes are served warm; one taste and you'll see what I mean.

SERVES 4 | PREP TIME: 30 MINUTES | COOK TIME: 35 MINUTES

2 handfuls of ice
4 medium eggs
4 plum tomatoes
sea salt
300g fine French beans, trimmed
400g small Charlotte potatoes, unpeeled and washed
2 thick-cut tuna steaks, 300g each (2.5cm thick)
olive oil, for rubbing
freshly ground black pepper
2 baby gem lettuces, leaves separated, washed and dried
a handful of pitted black olives
12 anchovy fillets, roughly chopped

FOR THE DRESSING
½ garlic clove, crushed
2 teaspoons Dijon mustard
1 tablespoon red wine vinegar
1 tablespoon water
2 tablespoons extra virgin olive oil
sea salt and freshly ground black pepper

Fill the sink or your largest bowl with cold water and add the ice. Bring two pans of water to the boil – one large, one small – then reboil the kettle. Carefully lower the eggs into the small pan, and when the water starts to boil, set a timer for 6 minutes. When the time is up, immediately remove the eggs from the water and put them straight into the ice bath to stop them from cooking further.

Meanwhile, make a small nick in each tomato, put them in a bowl and cover with boiling water. Leave for 30 seconds, then drain and drop them into the ice bath. Peel away the skins, cut into wedges and set aside.

Add salt to the water in the large pan, drop the beans in and boil for 3 minutes, then remove from the pan and immediately give them the ice bath treatment. Once they've cooled, drain them and pat dry on kitchen paper. Boil the potatoes in the same pan for 15–20 minutes or until just cooked through, then drain in a colander and leave to steam. Peel the skins and cover the potatoes with foil to keep warm.

Remove the eggs from the ice bath, tap to crack the shells, then very gently roll them on a chopping board. Peel them underwater; all the small shell fragments will sink. Remove and set aside.

Combine the dressing ingredients in a bowl, whisk together and season to taste.

Preheat the barbecue for direct grilling (see page 11). Rub the tuna steaks with olive oil and season. Sear on the grill for 1 ½ minutes on each side, then transfer to a plate to rest.

Put the tomatoes, lettuce, beans, olives and anchovies into a large bowl and spoon over half the dressing. Toss gently to coat, then divide between four salad bowls or plates.

Halve or quarter the warm potatoes, pour over a little dressing and toss to coat; doing this while they're still warm is one of the best parts of this dish. The potatoes suck up the dressing and are a lovely contrast to the cold elements of the salad. Nestle the potatoes between the leaves, then slice the eggs in half and lay on top. Slice the tuna against the grain, lay on top of the salad and finish with a drizzle of the remaining dressing.

TANDOORI SEA BREAM
with CHOPPED KACHUMBA

This is inspired by a meal my wife Holly and I had in India, sat on rickety chairs on a rooftop in Jaipur, balancing bags of salty masala fish on our knees, drinking cold beers and chewing on the tiny local lemons. Partly because of the setting, but also because of the wonderful simplicity of the food, the flavour of that delicately spiced fish will always stay with me.

SERVES 4 | PREP TIME: 25 MINUTES PLUS MARINATING | COOK TIME: 20 MINUTES

4 sea bream, weighing approx.
  450g each, gutted, scaled
  and left whole
vegetable oil, in a spray bottle

FOR THE MARINADE
4 garlic cloves, peeled
thumb-sized piece of
  fresh ginger, peeled
  and roughly chopped
juice of 1 lemon
2 teaspoons chilli powder
2 teaspoons garam masala
1 teaspoon ground cumin
1 teaspoon fine sea salt
100g thick Greek yogurt

FOR THE KACHUMBA
3 large, ripe tomatoes,
  deseeded and finely chopped
1 red onion, finely chopped
½ cucumber, peeled, deseeded
  and finely chopped
1 green chilli, finely chopped
juice of 1 lime
½ teaspoon garam masala
1 small bunch of coriander,
  finely chopped
sea salt and freshly ground
  black pepper

lemon wedges, to serve

Using a very sharp knife, score the fish skin a few times on both sides, then lay on a large baking tray. Put the marinade ingredients into a food processor and blend until smooth. Pour the marinade over the fish and rub it all over, working it into the cavity and the skin. Cover the tray with clingfilm and marinate in the fridge for 30 minutes.

Meanwhile, combine the kachumba ingredients in a bowl and season to taste.

Remove the fish from the fridge and preheat the barbecue for direct grilling (see page 11). Shake any excess marinade from the fish and lightly spray with vegetable oil. Lay on the grill and cook for 6–8 minutes. Turn, close the lid and cook for a further 6–8 minutes. Serve with the kachumba and lemon wedges.

SEA BASS, IBIZA STYLE

Early on a Tuesday morning the stalls in Ibiza town market are groaning with a stunning array of freshly caught fish. It's an exciting place and just makes me want to cook that beautifully fresh fish as simply as possible. My fish of choice tends to be the huge wild sea bass and I can't resist the lightly charred crispy skin that comes from barbecuing. Once the fish is on the grill, the key is to handle it as little as possible and only turn it when it's ready.

SERVES 6 | PREP TIME: 15 MINUTES | COOK TIME: ABOUT 10 MINUTES PLUS RESTING

1 large sea bass, weighing approx. 1.8–2kg, gutted, scaled and filleted
olive oil, for rubbing
sea salt flakes

FOR THE FENNEL SALAD
finely grated zest and juice of 1 unwaxed lemon
3 fennel bulbs
2 Granny Smith apples
½ quantity Pink Pickled Onions (page 126)
pinch of fine sea salt

Salsa Verde (page 129), to serve

Pat the fish dry with plenty of kitchen paper; it's essential that the skin is bone dry to ensure that it turns really crispy during cooking. Lay the fish on a wire rack and chill, uncovered, while you make the salad; the cool, dry air in the fridge will help to dry the skin further.

Put the lemon zest and juice in a large bowl. Remove the green fronds from the fennel bulbs and set aside. Using a mandoline, shave the bulbs into wafer-thin slices. As you slice the fennel, add it straight to the bowl with the lemon juice to stop it turning brown. Core the apples and finely slice on the mandoline, immediately adding to the bowl with the fennel. Toss through the Pink Pickled Onions and season with the salt. Just before serving, tear the fennel fronds into small pieces and toss through the salad.

Preheat the barbecue for direct grilling (see page 11). Score the fish at regular intervals with a very sharp knife, then rub with olive oil. Season with plenty of sea salt, then lay skin-side down on the grill. If your fish is really fresh (as it should be), it'll start to arch up when it hits the grill. As it does this, press down on the flesh; the aim is to ensure that all the skin is in contact with the grill. Now do nothing for a few minutes. If you try to move the fish, the skin will stick to the grill and separate from the flesh. Keep an eye on the flesh side; you'll see that the outer edges will turn white as the fish cooks. Once the white edges almost meet in the middle, carefully lift the fish with a couple of palette knives or fish slices. If it lifts easily, the fish is ready to turn. If it's still sticking slightly, leave it for another minute or so. Turn the fish and cook for a further 2–3 minutes, then remove from the grill.

A sea bass of this size is a meaty fish, so leave it to rest for a few minutes before serving. Place on a large platter in the centre of the table with the fennel salad and Salsa Verde.

TERIYAKI SALMON

The salty–sweet balance of teriyaki lends itself to rich, oily fish such as salmon. The marinade, which doubles as the sticky glaze, is incredibly easy to make and far better than the ready-made stuff. Keep an eye on the sauce as it reduces because it can quickly go too far and burn the sugar. Use a Japanese soy sauce rather than Chinese, which tends to be saltier.

SERVES 4 | PREP TIME: 10 MINUTES PLUS MARINATING | COOK TIME: ABOUT 10 MINUTES

500g centre-cut piece of
 salmon fillet, skin on,
 pin bones removed
vegetable oil, for rubbing

FOR THE MARINADE
150ml Japanese dark soy
 sauce (tamari)
100ml mirin
100ml sake
3 tablespoons golden
 caster sugar
2 garlic cloves, peeled
 and bashed
thumb-sized piece of fresh
 ginger, peeled and sliced

TO SERVE
1 tablespoon Japanese
 red pickled ginger
4 spring onions, finely
 shredded
2 teaspoons toasted
 sesame seeds

Score the skin of the salmon with a sharp knife at regular intervals, then lay in a dish just big enough to hold it. Place in the fridge, uncovered, while you make the marinade.

Combine the marinade ingredients in a saucepan and bring to the boil, then reduce the heat and simmer gently for 15 minutes until syrupy, stirring regularly. Strain through a sieve into a bowl and leave to cool to room temperature.

Pour the marinade over the salmon, toss to coat and return to the fridge for a couple of hours.

Preheat the barbecue for direct grilling (see page 11). Remove the salmon from the fridge, lift out of the marinade and pat dry. Pour the marinade into a saucepan and transfer to the grill to reheat. Rub the salmon with vegetable oil, lay skin-side down on the grill and cook for 3 minutes, then turn and cook for a further 3–4 minutes. Now baste the salmon with the marinade, brushing regularly for the final couple of minutes. Once the salmon is just cooked through, remove from the grill and brush with the remaining marinade. Scatter over the pickled ginger, spring onions and sesame seeds, then serve.

VARIATION: Swap the salmon for 500g free-range skinless chicken thigh fillets, cut into bite-sized pieces and thread onto metal skewers, or wooden skewers soaked in warm water for at least an hour. Marinate as above. Grill for 8–10 minutes, turning regularly, until cooked through and lightly charred.

MACKEREL with SEAWEED and MUSHROOM SALAD

As mackerel is such an oily fish it grills beautifully with little danger of drying out and its robust flavour deals well with a bit of smoke. You'll have to hunt down the shichimi togarashi (Japanese seven-spice powder) and the seaweed, but they keep for a couple of months once opened so are worth a trip to a Japanese shop or some online browsing.

SERVES 4 | PREP TIME: 15 MINUTES PLUS COOLING | COOK TIME: ABOUT 10 MINUTES

4 large, really fresh mackerel, weighing about 350g each, gutted and filleted
fine sea salt
shichimi togarashi, for seasoning

FOR THE SALAD
400g mixed mushrooms, such as enoki, shiitake and shimeji, larger ones sliced
2 garlic cloves, thinly sliced
400ml water
200ml rice vinegar
150ml light soy sauce
75g caster sugar
a small handful of dried wakame seaweed, rehydrated in cold water for 5 minutes then drained
1 cucumber, peeled, deseeded and sliced

You will need 16 wooden skewers, soaked in warm water for at least an hour.

For the salad, put the mushrooms and garlic in a large bowl. Combine the water, vinegar, soy and sugar in a saucepan and bring to the boil. Cook for 2 minutes, stirring occasionally, until the sugar has completely dissolved then pour the liquid over the mushrooms and garlic and stir to combine. Leave to cool completely, then drain and reserve the liquid. Add the seaweed and cucumber to the mushrooms and garlic, toss to combine and add a little of the reserved liquid to taste.

Preheat the barbecue for direct grilling (see page 11). Lightly score the mackerel skin at regular intervals, then thread each fillet lengthways onto two skewers (this will make them easier to handle during cooking). Season with salt and shichimi togarashi. Grill skin-side down for 3–4 minutes. Turn and cook for a minute or so, then remove from the heat and serve with the salad.

SQUID with THREE SALTS

The key to cooking great squid is to ensure that they are as fresh as possible. They should have a vibrant pink or purple mottling and bright, shiny eyes. Make sure your barbecue is screaming hot; squid need to be cooked hard and fast, just long enough to get a light char on the edges but not so long that they start to overcook. A couple of minutes is usually enough; as soon as the larger pieces curl up, it's ready. You'll have plenty of each salt left over, so store them in small airtight containers and use with grilled fish or steak.

SERVES 4 | PREP TIME: 20 MINUTES PLUS DRYING | COOK TIME: 2–3 MINUTES

4 large squid, cleaned, tubes
  and tentacles separated
olive oil, for coating

FOR THE CITRUS SALT
finely grated zest of
  ½ unwaxed lemon
finely grated zest of
  ½ pink grapefruit
2 tablespoons sea salt flakes

**FOR THE CHILLI AND
GARLIC SALT**
1 red bird's eye chilli,
  roughly chopped
1 small garlic clove, peeled
2 tablespoons sea salt flakes

**FOR THE SZECHUAN
SEAWEED SALT**
1 teaspoon Szechuan
  peppercorns
1 tablespoon dried
  wakame seaweed
2 tablespoons sea salt flakes

lemon and lime wedges,
  to serve

For the citrus salt, put the zests and half the salt into a mortar and grind to a fine paste with a pestle. Add the remaining salt and rub together lightly with your fingertips to mix. Spread onto a plate and leave to dry at room temperature for 3–4 hours.

For the chilli and garlic salt, put the chilli, garlic and half the salt into the mortar and grind to a fine paste with the pestle. Add the remaining salt and rub together lightly with your fingertips to mix. Spread onto a plate and leave to dry at room temperature for 3–4 hours.

For the Szechuan seaweed salt, put the peppercorns, seaweed and half the salt into the mortar and grind to a fine powder with the pestle. Add the remaining salt and rub together lightly with your fingertips to mix.

Preheat the barbecue for direct grilling (see page 11). Using a sharp knife, cut down the side of each squid tube and open out to make a flat piece. Scrape clean with the side of a spoon, then lightly score the flesh in a diamond pattern with your knife.

Toss the squid tubes and tentacles in a little olive oil, then divide into three equal piles. Lightly season the squid, using a different salt for each, then grill for 2–3 minutes. The tentacles will cook very quickly, so they'll need to come off first, and the tubes will take a minute or so longer. As soon as the squid is cooked, slice the tubes into bite-sized pieces and serve with the salts and lemon and lime wedges.

SEPIA a la PLANCHA

When you think of breakfast, sepia (cuttlefish) with garlic and parsley probably isn't the first thing that comes to mind. However, for years in a small café on the edge of Ibiza town market they've been serving this up to local old boys playing dominoes and drinking sherry, or market traders grabbing a quick bite to eat. Cuttlefish can be messy to prepare, so tackle the job in a large sink to contain the ink that'll invariably squirt all over the place.

SERVES 4 │ PREP TIME: 15 MINUTES │ COOK TIME: 5 MINUTES PLUS WARMING

2 large cuttlefish,
    cleaned and prepared
olive oil, for coating
    and brushing
sea salt flakes
2 fat garlic cloves,
    roughly chopped
1 small bunch of flat-
    leaf parsley, leaves
    finely chopped

TO SERVE
lemon wedges
crusty bread

Preheat the barbecue for direct grilling (see page 11). Slice the cuttlefish in half lengthways and scrape the inside of the tubes clean with the side of a spoon. Lightly score the inside of the tubes with a knife in a crisscross pattern, taking care not to cut all the way through.

Pour a glug of oil into a large bowl (ideally a metal one) and leave in a warm place – either next to the barbecue or in the sunshine if the weather is being kind.

Brush the cuttlefish with olive oil, season with plenty of salt and then grill for 2 minutes on each side until lightly golden around the edges. Transfer to the bowl with the warmed oil, add the garlic and parsley and toss to coat. Leave the cuttlefish to rest for a couple of minutes before serving with lemon wedges and crusty bread.

COAL-ROAST SEA BASS
with MUSSELS

I've cooked plenty of meat 'dirty' style – directly on the coals – but fish is far more delicate
and therefore needs some special attention. Ask your fishmonger to gut the fish but to leave
on the scales to protect the sweet flesh underneath while it cooks on the coals, imparting
a fantastic smoky flavour. Ensure that the coals are glowing nicely: too hot and the fish
will burn before it's fully cooked; too cold and the fish will steam and fall apart.

SERVES 4 | PREP TIME: 15 MINUTES | COOK TIME: 20 MINUTES

2 sea bass, weighing 750g
  each, gutted, scales on
  and left whole
sea salt flakes
1kg mussels, cleaned
  (discard any that don't
  close when tapped sharply
  on the work surface)
dash of dry white wine
1 garlic clove, crushed
knob of unsalted butter

TO SERVE
750g baby new potatoes,
  unpeeled and washed
sea salt
Salsa Verde (page 129) or
  Mayonnaise flavoured with
  roasted garlic (page 131)
1 small bunch of flat-leaf
  parsley, finely chopped

Preheat the barbecue and remove the grill; you'll need plenty
of charcoal for this recipe, as the fish need to be buried. Pat the
insides of the fish dry with kitchen paper and season generously
with sea salt flakes. Make a large foil parcel, add the mussels,
wine, garlic and butter and seal tightly.

Rake the coals to one side of the barbecue, leaving a thin layer
on the bottom. Lay the fish straight onto the coals, then shovel the
remaining coals on top; the fish should be completely covered.
Rest the foil parcel on the coals and cook for 10–12 minutes.

Meanwhile, cook the potatoes in a saucepan of boiling salted
water for about 15 minutes until soft, then drain.

To check that the mussels are cooked, carefully open one
side of the foil parcel; if the shells have all opened, they're ready
(throw out any odd ones that haven't opened). The fish is slightly
trickier to check for doneness: carefully scrape back the coals
and, using a small, sharp knife, push back the flesh at the thickest
part (just behind the head); the flesh should be white and just
cooked through. If it's not quite ready, cover with the coals
and cook for a further couple of minutes.

To serve, lightly crush the potatoes with the back of a fork
and tip into a warm serving bowl with the Salsa Verde or
garlic Mayonnaise. Open the foil parcel, pour the mussels
and cooking liquid over the potatoes and toss to combine.
Scatter over the parsley.

Carefully scrape back the coals and lift the fish onto a serving
board, dusting off any ash as you go. Take the fish to the table,
peel back the burnt skin and discard. Use a fish slice or palette
knife to separate the flesh from the bones and serve with the
mussels and potatoes.

LOBSTER ROLLS

This is a seriously delicious way to serve lobster – piled up in a toasted potato roll, dripping with butter. I first tasted this in New York, at a great seafood restaurant called Catch. Make sure you have everything else ready before grilling the lobster so that you can dress the meat as soon as it's cooked.

SERVES 4 | PREP TIME: 20 MINUTES PLUS FREEZING | COOK TIME: 15 MINUTES

2 live lobsters, weighing approx. 900g each
4 tablespoons melted unsalted butter
6 tablespoons Mayonnaise (page 131)
2 tablespoons finely chopped chives
1 tablespoon finely chopped tarragon
1 teaspoon Dijon mustard
pinch of hot smoked paprika
sea salt and freshly ground black pepper
4 Potato Rolls (page 115)
2 baby gem lettuces, leaves separated, washed and dried

Preheat the barbecue for direct grilling (see page 11). To kill the lobsters humanely, put them in the freezer for an hour to render them unconscious. Remove from the freezer and cover them with a couple of cold, wet tea towels, leaving the heads exposed. Push the tip of a large, sharp knife through the cross on the top of the head; do this in one swift, purposeful movement to kill the lobster instantly.

Cut the lobsters in half lengthways and brush the cut sides with some of the melted butter. Grill the lobsters cut-side down for 5 minutes, then turn, brush with more butter and cook for a further 5 minutes. Twist off the tails and remove from the grill, leaving the claws to grill for a further 2–3 minutes. Pull the meat from the tails and roughly chop. Crack the claws with a sharp knife or lobster cracker, pull out the meat and roughly chop.

Mix together the Mayonnaise, herbs, mustard and paprika in a large bowl, add the lobster and toss gently to coat. Season to taste.

Cut the Potato Rolls in half lengthways, brush the cut sides with the remaining melted butter and toast on the barbecue for a couple of minutes until golden. Pile the lobster and lettuce into the rolls and serve.

VEGGIES, SIDES & SLAWS

GRILLED PANZANELLA

This classic Italian salad is the perfect dish for celebrating sweet, ripe tomatoes; use a mixture of colours and shapes and buy the very best you can. Lightly charring the tomatoes introduces a subtle smoky flavour that works brilliantly with the peppery olive oil and fresh basil. This isn't a salad to make too far in advance; it needs to sit just long enough for the flavours to marry together, but not so long that the bread turns to mush.

SERVES 6 AS A SIDE | PREP TIME: 15 MINUTES PLUS COOLING | COOK TIME: 30 MINUTES

6 tablespoons extra virgin
   olive oil
2 garlic cloves, crushed
200g day-old white bread,
   torn into small chunks
2 red onions, finely sliced
2 red chillies, roughly chopped
large pinch of sea salt flakes
1 red pepper
1 yellow pepper
1kg ripe mixed tomatoes
2 tablespoons sherry vinegar
1 small bunch of basil,
   leaves torn

Preheat the oven to 180°C/gas mark 4. Whisk half the oil with the garlic in a bowl, add the bread and toss to coat. Tip onto a baking tray and bake for 10–15 minutes until golden.

Meanwhile, put the onions and chillies in a large bowl, add the salt and toss to coat. Gently knead and toss the onions and chillies together for a couple of minutes until softened, then drain off any excess liquid.

Preheat the barbecue for direct grilling (see page 11). Lay the peppers on the grill and cook for about 10 minutes until blackened and charred all over, turning regularly. Transfer the peppers to a bowl, cover with clingfilm and leave to cool and steam for 10 minutes. When cool enough to handle, rub the skins away, discard the stalks and seeds and tear into long strips. Add to the onions and chillies.

While the peppers are cooling, lightly char the tomatoes on the grill for a few minutes, turning regularly. Roughly chop and add to the bowl. Whisk together the remaining oil and the vinegar, pour over the salad and toss to coat. Toss through the bread and basil and leave to stand for 10 minutes before serving; the bread should be starting to soften by this point but still retain a bit of crunch.

CHARRED CORN with SMOKED CHILLI BUTTER

Sweet and smoky corn on the cob is the ultimate barbecue side dish: cheap, quick and easy to prepare and, most importantly, it can be eaten with your hands. I cook mine directly on the coals so that the husks act as a protective layer, allowing the corn to steam and soften gently. Towards the end of cooking, as the husks burn away, the corn will start to lightly char and take on a delicious smoky flavour. If you can't find corn cobs in their husks, use peeled cobs individually wrapped in a single layer of foil.

SERVES 4 AS A SIDE | **PREP TIME: 5 MINUTES PLUS SOAKING** | **COOK TIME: 15 MINUTES**

2 dried chipotle chillies
½ teaspoon chilli flakes
1 garlic clove, crushed
finely grated zest of
   1 unwaxed lime
100g salted butter,
   at room temperature
good pinch of fine sea salt
4 sweetcorn cobs in
   their husks

Preheat the barbecue for direct grilling (see page 11). Soak the chillies in boiling water for 10 minutes until soft, then drain and leave to cool. Chop finely and put into a bowl with the chilli flakes, garlic, lime zest and butter. Beat together until smooth.

Bring a large pan of water to the boil, throw in the salt and add the sweetcorn cobs in their husks. Cook for 3 minutes, then drain.

To cook the sweetcorn directly on the coals, remove the grill and rake the coals into an even layer. Lay the sweetcorn on the coals and cook for 10 minutes, turning regularly. The husks will catch fire occasionally, so keep them moving to reduce the risk of flames to a minimum. Remove from the heat and when cool enough to handle peel away the charred husks. Serve with the smoked chilli butter.

If you're using a gas barbecue, or prefer not to cook directly on the coals, the sweetcorn will need an extra 5 minutes.

CHARGRILLED LEAVES
with BURNT LEMON DRESSING

Grilling salad leaves might seem a little unusual, but, trust me, this tastes fantastic.
Adding heat to robust leaves intensifies their flavour and adds a subtle smokiness
to the dish. The dressing is one of my all-time favourites; be generous with it and
mop the plate clean with crusty bread.

SERVES 6 | PREP TIME: 15 MINUTES | COOK TIME: 15 MINUTES

FOR THE DRESSING
1 unwaxed lemon
100ml buttermilk
1 tablespoon Mayonnaise
   (page 131)
1 tablespoon extra virgin
   olive oil
1 small garlic clove, crushed
pinch of caster sugar
sea salt and freshly ground
   black pepper

FOR THE SALAD
2 heads of red chicory,
   halved lengthways
2 heads of white chicory,
   halved lengthways
4 baby gem lettuces,
   halved lengthways
olive oil, for brushing
2 red chillies, deseeded
   (optional) and finely
   chopped

crusty bread, to serve

Preheat the barbecue for direct grilling (see page 11). For the
dressing, finely grate the lemon zest and add to the buttermilk,
Mayonnaise, oil, garlic and sugar in a bowl, then whisk together
until thickened.

Halve the lemon and place cut-side down on the grill for
2–3 minutes until lightly charred and caramelised, then set
aside to cool. Once the lemon is cool enough to handle, squeeze
the juice into the bowl with the dressing, whisk to combine
and season to taste.

For the salad, brush the chicory and baby gem halves with
a little olive oil and lay cut-side down on the grill. Cook the baby
gem for 2–3 minutes on each side and the chicory for a couple
of minutes longer; the leaves should be charred and started
to wilt but retain plenty of crunch.

Cut the roots away from the baby gem and chicory, separate
into individual leaves and put into a large bowl. Pour over the
dressing and toss lightly to coat the leaves. Scatter over the
chopped chillies and serve with crusty bread.

SPICED CAULIFLOWER STEAKS
with **YOGURT** and **TAHINI DRESSING**

Vegetarians often get a raw deal at barbecues, and there is nothing sadder than a limp veggie burger banished to one side of the grill. But vegetables can be the star of the show, and here the humble cauliflower is transformed into something seriously delicious.

SERVES 4 | PREP TIME: 10 MINUTES PLUS MARINATING | COOK TIME: 15 MINUTES

2 large cauliflowers
2 tablespoons extra virgin
    olive oil, plus extra to finish
1 tablespoon ras el hanout
1 teaspoon fine sea salt
2 garlic cloves, crushed

FOR THE DRESSING
4 tablespoons Greek yogurt
2 tablespoons tahini
1 tablespoon extra virgin
    olive oil
squeeze of lemon juice
sea salt and freshly ground
    black pepper

TO SERVE
a small handful of
    pomegranate seeds
1 small bunch of coriander,
    roughly chopped

Slice two thick slices from the centre of each cauliflower, cutting from top to bottom, to make four thick steaks about 3cm thick, then lay in a large tray. Whisk together the oil, ras el hanout, salt and garlic, then pour over the cauliflower and toss to coat. Cover with clingfilm and marinate in the fridge for 2 hours.

Meanwhile, whisk together the ingredients for the dressing, adding enough water to loosen to a pouring consistency. Season to taste and set aside.

Preheat the barbecue for direct grilling (see page 11). Grill the cauliflower steaks for 10 minutes until lightly charred and starting to soften, turning regularly. Remove from the grill, wrap in foil and cook for a further 5 minutes.

Arrange the cauliflower on a serving platter, drizzle with the dressing and scatter over the pomegranate seeds and coriander. To finish, drizzle over a little extra virgin olive oil.

NOTE: You'll end up with some leftover cauliflower, so season lightly with salt, char on the barbecue and break into florets. Dip in Baba Ganoush (page 120), Tzatziki (page 122) or Mayonnaise flavoured with roasted garlic (page 131).

BUTTERMILK ONION RINGS

Crunchy fried onion rings go brilliantly with barbecued meat; either inside my Chilli Cheese Burgers (page 42) or alongside Pulled Pork (page 142) or Brisket (page 134). Soaking in milk helps to soften the onions and remove any harshness before frying.

SERVES 4 AS A SIDE | **PREP TIME: 10 MINUTES PLUS STANDING** | **COOK TIME: ABOUT 10 MINUTES**

2 large onions
500ml whole milk
200ml buttermilk
2 medium eggs
1 tablespoon Hot Sauce
   (page 128) or Tabasco sauce
150g plain flour
1 teaspoon cayenne pepper
1 teaspoon ground
   white pepper
1 teaspoon fine sea salt,
   plus extra for seasoning
   after frying
vegetable oil, for deep-frying

Peel the onions, slice horizontally into 1cm-thick rounds and separate into rings. Put the onion rings into a bowl, cover with the milk and set aside for 15 minutes.

Whisk together the buttermilk, eggs and Hot Sauce in a jug, then pour into a shallow bowl. Combine the flour, cayenne pepper, white pepper and salt in a separate shallow bowl.

Preheat the oil in a deep fryer or deep saucepan to 170°C and line a plate or baking tray with kitchen paper. Drain the onion rings and, working in batches, toss them in the seasoned flour, then in the buttermilk mixture and finally dust with another coating of flour. (If you're also planning on making the Mac 'n' Cheese (opposite), save the milk from soaking the onions to use in the cheese sauce.) Fry, in batches, for 2–3 minutes until golden and crisp, then remove from the oil, drain on kitchen paper and season with salt.

MAC 'N' CHEESE

Growing up as a child of the 80s when mac 'n' cheese was a family comfort food staple, it does seem slightly odd that it's now seen a huge resurgence in restaurants all over the world. It's easy to see why; it's bloody delicious. What makes it particularly appealing to chefs is its versatility, providing the opportunity to showboat with the inclusion of high-end ingredients such as lobster and fresh truffle. The juxtaposition of homely cheesy pasta and luxury ingredients is clearly too much to resist. Call me old-fashioned, but I prefer my mac straight up; pasta in a rich, silky cheese sauce with a bubbling crust that everyone will fight over. If you're planning a bit of a pig-out, serve this alongside Brisket (page 134) or Pulled Pork (page 142), with a few gherkins to cut through the richness.

SERVES 6 AS A SIDE | PREP TIME: 10 MINUTES | COOK TIME: 30 MINUTES PLUS STANDING

fine sea salt
500g dried elbow macaroni
500ml whole milk
1 onion, peeled and quartered
2 garlic cloves, peeled
    and bashed
pinch of ground nutmeg
pinch of ground white pepper
50g unsalted butter
50g plain flour
1 tablespoon Dijon mustard
300g mature Cheddar
    cheese, grated
75g Parmesan cheese,
    finely grated

Preheat the oven to 200°C/gas mark 6. Bring a large pan of salted water to the boil, add the pasta and cook for a couple of minutes shy of the cooking time specified on the packet. Drain, refresh under cold running water and set aside.

While the pasta is cooking, heat the milk, onion, garlic, nutmeg and white pepper in a small saucepan until simmering, then cover and remove from the heat. Leave to stand for 10 minutes before fishing out the onion and garlic with a slotted spoon.

In a separate pan, melt the butter and whisk in the flour. Cook for 2–3 minutes, stirring, until the mixture starts to turn a light brown colour. Gradually whisk in the milk; don't add too much at once, otherwise the sauce will turn lumpy. Once all the milk has been incorporated, bring the sauce to a simmer and cook gently for 2 minutes, whisking constantly. Remove the pan from the heat and whisk in the mustard and most of the Cheddar, reserving a handful for the top.

Add the macaroni to the sauce and stir until evenly coated. Pour the mixture into a large ovenproof dish and scatter the Parmesan and remaining Cheddar over the top. Bake for 20 minutes until the cheese is golden brown and bubbling. Remove from the oven and leave to stand for a few minutes before serving.

CHIPOTLE SLAW

This slaw is fresh, vibrant and has a smoky heat from the chipotle chilli paste.
It goes beautifully with rich, smoked recipes such as the Smoked Chicken (page 136),
Beef Short Ribs (page 18) and Pulled Pork (page 142).

SERVES 6 AS A SIDE │ PREP TIME: 15 MINUTES PLUS CHILLING

1 small red cabbage
6 spring onions,
   finely shredded
2 carrots, peeled and
   coarsely grated
2 teaspoons chipotle paste
juice of 1–2 limes
sea salt
1 small bunch of coriander,
   leaves chopped

Quarter the cabbage, remove the tough white core and finely shred the rest. Put the cabbage into a large bowl with the spring onions, carrots and chipotle paste and toss to combine.

Add the lime juice and salt to taste, cover the bowl with clingfilm and chill in the fridge for an hour; this will give enough time for the lime juice and salt to start to soften the vegetables.

Remove from the fridge and allow to come back to room temperature. Stir through the chopped coriander and serve.

ROAST RADISHES
with CRUMBLED PARMESAN

Crunchy, peppery radishes and salty, tangy Parmesan cheese go brilliantly together.
And so they should; they're essentially salt and pepper in fancy clothes. I first tried this
combination at The Standard Grill in New York, where they served chunks of well-aged
Parmesan alongside chilled breakfast radishes. Adding a little heat and smoke intensifies
the flavour of the radishes and starts to gently melt the Parmesan.

SERVES 4 AS A SIDE | PREP TIME: 5 MINUTES | COOK TIME: 10 MINUTES

400g firm radishes
2 teaspoons olive oil
1 tablespoon honey
1 tablespoon sherry vinegar
sea salt and freshly ground
    black pepper
30g aged Parmesan
    cheese, crumbled

Preheat the barbecue for direct grilling (see page 11). Wash
the radishes and remove the leaves, leaving about 1cm of stalk
on each. Whisk together the oil, honey and vinegar in a large
bowl, season and set aside.

Grill the radishes directly on the grill for 8–10 minutes until
lightly charred and starting to soften, turning regularly. Keep
the bowl of dressing next to the barbecue, and as soon as the
radishes are cooked, transfer them straight to the dressing.
Toss the hot radishes in the dressing, then tip them onto
a serving plate and scatter over the Parmesan.

ULTIMATE POTATO SALAD

I've played around with this recipe over the years, trying different types of potatoes, dressings and herbs in an effort to come up with the best combination. I'm pretty sure I've nailed it with this one. The secret to a great potato salad is dressing the potatoes while they're warm; as they cool they'll soak up the mayonnaise and will taste all the better for it.

SERVES 6 AS A SIDE | **PREP TIME: 10 MINUTES PLUS COOLING** | **COOK TIME: 15–20 MINUTES**

fine sea salt
1kg baby new potatoes,
    unpeeled and washed
4 tablespoons Mayonnaise
    (page 131)
1 tablespoon crème fraîche
1 tablespoon wholegrain
    mustard
2 teaspoons Dijon mustard
1 tablespoon extra virgin
    olive oil
2 teaspoons white wine vinegar
6 spring onions, finely sliced
8 cornichons, finely chopped
1 tablespoon small capers,
    drained
1 small bunch of flat-leaf
    parsley, leaves finely chopped
1 small bunch of tarragon,
    leaves finely chopped
freshly ground black pepper

Bring a large pan of salted water to the boil, add the potatoes and simmer for 15–20 minutes until tender and the skins are starting to split.

Meanwhile, whisk together the Mayonnaise, crème fraîche, mustards, oil and vinegar in a large bowl.

Drain the potatoes, reserving a little of the cooking water, and leave in the colander for a couple of minutes to cool slightly. Halve the warm potatoes and add to the mayonnaise mixture along with a couple of spoonfuls of the reserved cooking water. Toss to combine, then set aside to cool to room temperature.

Once cool, stir through the remaining ingredients and season to taste.

GRILLED RED CABBAGE
with **HOT** and **SOUR DRESSING**

Red cabbage is fantastically versatile and works well pickled, braised or shredded in a slaw. If you've never tried grilling it, you're missing out on a treat. The key is to ensure that each wedge of cabbage is cut through the core to stop it falling apart during cooking.

SERVES 4–6 AS A SIDE | **PREP TIME: 5 MINUTES** | **COOK TIME: 15–20 MINUTES**

1 red cabbage
olive oil, for brushing
sea salt and freshly ground
   black pepper
1 small bunch of coriander,
   leaves torn

FOR THE DRESSING
2 tablespoons sriracha
   chilli sauce
juice of 1 lime
1 tablespoon honey
½ teaspoon toasted
   sesame oil

Preheat the barbecue for direct grilling (see page 11). Cut the cabbage into 12 wedges, keeping the core intact so that they hold together. Brush on both sides with olive oil and season. Grill for 15–20 minutes, turning occasionally, until just cooked through. To test if the cabbage wedges are cooked, insert a small, sharp knife into the thickest part; it should go through with little resistance.

Meanwhile, whisk together the ingredients for the dressing.

Arrange the cabbage wedges on a large serving plate, drizzle over the dressing and scatter over the torn coriander leaves.

TABBOULEH

This Middle Eastern salad is immensely popular and, as a result, is frequently ruined by too much bulgar wheat (or, in the worst case, heaps of couscous) and not enough herbs. Proper tabbouleh should be a fresh, intensely flavoured herb salad with a hint of bulgar wheat, not the other way around. Don't be tempted to make this too far in advance; it's the potent flavour and freshness that goes so well with smoky grilled meat, fish and vegetables.

SERVES 4 | PREP TIME: 15 MINUTES PLUS STANDING

3 tablespoons fine
    bulgar wheat
3 tablespoons extra virgin
    olive oil
juice of 2 lemons
½ garlic clove, crushed
½ teaspoon ground cumin
½ teaspoon hot smoked paprika
½ teaspoon ground cinnamon
1 small white onion,
    finely chopped
300g ripe tomatoes,
    finely chopped
100g flat-leaf parsley,
    finely chopped
50g mint, finely chopped
sea salt and freshly ground
    black pepper

Put the bulgar wheat into a sieve and rinse under cold running water for a couple of minutes until the water runs clear.

Whisk together the oil, lemon juice, garlic and spices in a large bowl, then stir in the bulgar wheat. Leave to stand for 5 minutes before stirring in the remaining ingredients and seasoning to taste.

CHICKPEA, ROAST PEPPER and CHORIZO SALAD

Simple to prepare, big on flavour and a real showstopper, this dish is perfect for feeding – and impressing – a large crowd. The salad is something I regularly make in Ibiza, where the peppers and chorizo are the best I've ever tasted. My greengrocer, Juan, has a forager working for him who often comes back with bags of giant wild rocket; really peppery and a far cry from the pre-packed stuff. However, I don't expect you to go trudging through the hills to find this stuff, so a good peppery salad rocket will work just fine.

SERVES 8 | PREP TIME: 10 MINUTES | COOK TIME: 20 MINUTES

3 large red peppers
1 garlic bulb
olive oil, for drizzling
400g Iberico chorizo, peeled and halved lengthways
1 quantity Pink Pickled Onions (page 126)
3 x 400g jars Spanish chickpeas, drained
2 tablespoons extra virgin olive oil
2 tablespoons sherry vinegar
200g rocket leaves

Preheat the barbecue for direct grilling (see page 11) and remove the grill. Bury the peppers in the hot coals, replace the grill and leave the peppers to cook for 10 minutes. If you're cooking on a gas barbecue, grill the peppers for 15 minutes over a high heat, tunring regularly until blistered and blackened.

Meanwhile, drizzle the garlic bulb with olive oil, wrap in foil and lay on the grill.

Once the time is up for the peppers, lift the grill off and pull them from the coals; they'll be jet black and will look like they're ruined, but don't worry. Replace the grill with the garlic bulb while you leave the peppers to cool, then rub away all the charred exterior and you'll be left with sweet, smoky flesh. Don't be tempted to rinse the peppers, as you'll wash away all the flavour. Discard the stalks and seeds and tear the flesh into strips.

Lay the chorizo on the grill and cook for 7–8 minutes, turning regularly until crisp. Remove from the grill, thinly slice and combine with the peppers, Pink Pickled Onions and chickpeas in a large bowl.

Remove the garlic from the grill, unwrap and squeeze the soft flesh from the cloves into a small bowl. Add the oil and vinegar and whisk together, then pour over the salad and toss to combine. Just before serving, toss through the rocket leaves.

FETA and CHILLI PARCELS with GREEK SALAD

Few recipes embody the brilliance of summer produce better than a Greek salad; sweet, sun-ripened tomatoes and crisp cucumber are crucial. Traditionally it's served with a single slab of feta on top, leaving you to crumble it through the salad as you go. I've also tried another equally simple, equally delicious dish of baked feta cooked in a wood-fired oven with a handful of green chillies. So this is my take on a summer classic, combining both recipes to make something really special.

SERVES 4 | PREP TIME: 15 MINUTES | COOK TIME: 15 MINUTES

olive oil, for greasing
    and drizzling
2 green chillies, finely sliced
2 x 200g blocks barrel-aged
    feta, drained
freshly ground black pepper

FOR THE SALAD
2 tablespoons extra virgin
    olive oil
1 tablespoon red wine vinegar
½ garlic clove, crushed
1 teaspoon dried oregano
1 small red onion, finely sliced
1 cucumber
4 ripe tomatoes
a large handful of Kalamata
    olives, pitted
sea salt and freshly ground
    black pepper

crusty bread, to serve

Preheat the barbecue for direct grilling (see page 11). Lightly oil a large sheet of foil, scatter over the sliced chillies and lay the feta on top. Drizzle with a little more oil and top with a few twists of pepper. Seal the foil into a parcel and lay on the grill. Cook for 15 minutes, turning occasionally.

Meanwhile, whisk together the oil, vinegar, garlic and oregano in a large bowl, add the onion and set aside while you prepare the rest of the salad. Roughly peel the cucumber, halve lengthways and scoop out the seeds with a teaspoon. Roughly chop and add to the bowl. Quarter the tomatoes, remove the tough cores and roughly chop, then add to the bowl. Add the olives, toss to combine and season to taste; the olives and feta should negate the need for much salt.

Unwrap the feta and serve with the salad and crusty bread.

BROCCOLI with GOCHUJANG and LEMON

This punchy little vegetable dish is basically a riff on the classic combination of broccoli, chilli and garlic. For the chilli element, I use gochujang, a rich, spicy, fermented Korean chilli paste with a brilliantly complex flavour that works in all sorts of dishes. Try hot, crispy chips dipped in gochujang mayo; filthy and delicious.

SERVES 4 AS A SIDE | PREP TIME: 5 MINUTES | COOK TIME: ABOUT 10 MINUTES

500g tenderstem broccoli
fine sea salt
2 tablespoons gochujang
    chilli paste
1 tablespoon rice vinegar
1 teaspoon toasted sesame oil
finely grated zest of
    2 unwaxed lemons
1 garlic clove, crushed
vegetable oil, for greasing
2 teaspoons toasted
    sesame seeds

Preheat the barbecue for direct grilling (see page 11). Bring a large pan of salted water to the boil, add the broccoli and blanch for 2 minutes. Drain and refresh under cold running water.

Combine the gochujang, vinegar, sesame oil, lemon zest and garlic in a large bowl and whisk until smooth.

Dip a wad of kitchen paper in vegetable oil and use a long pair of tongs to brush the grill with the oil. Grill the broccoli for 3–4 minutes, turning occasionally, until lightly charred and just cooked through.

Transfer the broccoli to the bowl with the dressing, toss to coat and then tip out onto a serving platter. Sprinkle over the sesame seeds and serve immediately.

NEW POTATOES
BAKED in a BAG

This is a great way of cooking potatoes on the barbecue and can easily be scaled up if you're feeding a large crowd. Make sure all the potatoes are roughly the same size – halve any larger ones if needed – so that they cook evenly. They take a little while to cook through, but if you leave the bag sealed, they'll stay warm while you cook the rest of your meal.

SERVES 4 AS A SIDE | PREP TIME: 5 MINUTES | COOK TIME: 40 MINUTES

500g baby new potatoes, unpeeled and washed, larger ones halved
6 unpeeled garlic cloves, bashed
2 bay leaves
1 tablespoon extra virgin olive oil
sea salt and freshly ground black pepper

Preheat the barbecue for direct grilling (see page 11).

Combine the ingredients in a large bowl. Take a large sheet of foil, about 50cm long, and fold it in half away from you. Fold the sides in to make a pouch, then open it out at the mouth; you should have a foil bag, open at the top. Tip the potatoes in and seal the top of the bag to make a neat parcel. Lay on the grill and cook for 40 minutes, turning every 10 minutes.

POTATO ROLLS

I've long searched for the perfect bread roll to go alongside barbecued food. On a recent trip to New York I discovered the answer: a soft, light roll, strong enough to contain any decent burger or hot dog yet without being dense or cloying. The secret ingredient? Mashed potato. It gives the rolls a great chewy softness with the same richness you get from brioche but not the overly sweet taste. Shape into long rolls for hot dogs (pages 47–48) or Lobster Rolls (page 87), or into traditional rounds for burgers (pages 42 and 56) or Pulled Pork (page 142).

MAKES 8 | PREP TIME: 20 MINUTES PLUS RISING | COOK TIME: 30 MINUTES

500g strong white bread flour
7g sachet fast-action dried yeast
50g caster sugar
100g cold mashed potato
2 teaspoons fine sea salt
200ml warm water
3 medium egg yolks
100g salted butter, softened
vegetable oil, for greasing
fine semolina, for dusting

FOR THE GLAZE
2 medium egg yolks
1 tablespoon whole milk
2 teaspoons vegetable oil

sesame seeds, for sprinkling
(if making Potato Buns –
see variation)

Put the flour, yeast and sugar into the bowl of a stand mixer fitted with a dough hook. In a separate bowl, combine the mashed potato, salt, water and egg yolks. Push the potato mixture through a fine-meshed sieve onto the flour mixture, then knead on a medium speed for 5 minutes.

Reduce the speed to its lowest setting and add the softened butter until it's all incorporated and you have a smooth, shiny dough. Tip into a lightly oiled bowl, cover with a clean tea towel and leave in a warm place for an hour or until doubled in size.

Weigh the dough – it should be roughly 1kg – then weigh the mixture into eight equal pieces. Weighing each piece guarantees that they'll turn out the same size and bake more evenly.

Roll each piece into an even 20cm-long sausage shape, then lay on a baking tray dusted with semolina. Continue with the remaining dough, leaving a 2cm gap between each roll; this is enough space for them to rise without merging into one giant mega roll, but close enough for them to just touch once risen, giving you that trademark batch-baked look. You may need two baking trays to ensure that the rolls are evenly spaced.

Once all the rolls are in place, cover loosely with clingfilm and set aside in a warm place to rise for a further 30 minutes.

Preheat the oven to 180°C/gas mark 4. Mix together the glaze ingredients in a small bowl and brush over the rolls. Using a very sharp knife, cut a shallow slit down the centre of the top of each roll, stopping 2cm short of each end. Bake for 30 minutes until golden brown, covering loosely with foil halfway through cooking to stop them from becoming too dark.

VARIATION: For **Potato Buns** for burgers (pages 42 and 56), make the dough as above but roll into eight equal balls and flatten slightly. Bake as above and sprinkle with a few sesame seeds when you glaze them.

FLATBREADS

You can't beat homemade flatbreads; beautifully soft and lightly charred, they're perfect for wrapping around Lamb Shish Kebabs (page 44) and Pork Souvlaki (page 57), or to serve alongside Baba Ganoush (page 120) and Tzatziki (page 122) for dipping. You can make these in advance too; keep them wrapped in a clean tea towel, then flash them over the barbecue to warm through just before serving.

MAKES 8 │ PREP TIME: 25 MINUTES PLUS PROVING │ COOK TIME: 15 MINUTES

500g strong white
   bread flour
7g sachet fast-action
   dried yeast
320ml water
2 tablespoons olive oil,
   plus extra for greasing
2 teaspoons fine sea salt
1 teaspoon caster sugar
fine semolina, for dusting

Tip the flour and yeast into the bowl of a stand mixer fitted with a dough hook. Whisk together the remaining ingredients (except the semolina) in a jug until the salt and sugar have dissolved. Start the machine on a medium speed and gradually add the liquid. Knead for 5 minutes, then turn the speed up a notch and knead for a further 5 minutes.

Tip the dough into a lightly oiled bowl, cover with a clean tea towel and leave in a warm place for an hour or until doubled in size.

Preheat the barbecue for direct grilling (see page 11) and lay a pizza stone or heavy baking tray on the grill. Divide the dough into eight equal pieces, then dust the work surface with semolina and roll each piece into a large, thin round.

Lay the flatbreads onto the hot pizza stone or baking tray, and cook for a couple of minutes on each side until puffed up and lightly charred. As soon as each flatbread is ready, transfer it to a plate and cover with a clean tea towel. This will trap any steam and soften the breads as they cool; otherwise you'll end up with really brittle breads – delicious, but impossible to use as a wrap.

VARIATION: If you want to eat the bread on its own, you can add extra flavours. Try adding the leaves of 3 sprigs of rosemary, finely chopped, and 75g finely grated Parmesan to the dough. Once they're cooked, brush them with a mixture of 1 crushed garlic clove and 45g softened salted butter.

SAUCES, DIPS & PICKLES

BABA GANOUSH

This smoky aubergine dish shows how a bit of smoke can transform a simple vegetable into something special. Once the aubergines have cooked and you've scraped away the burnt skin to reveal the sweet, smoky flesh, chop it by hand; don't use a food processor or you'll lose all that lovely texture and the aubergines will turn watery.

SERVES 4–6 AS A DIP OR SIDE │ PREP TIME: 10 MINUTES PLUS COOLING │ COOK TIME: 20 MINUTES

2 large aubergines
2 garlic cloves, peeled
    and halved lengthways
2 tablespoons tahini
juice of 1 lemon, plus
    extra if needed to taste
1 teaspoon sumac
sea salt

TO SERVE
Flatbreads (page 117)

Preheat the barbecue for direct grilling (see page 11). Cut a slit in the side of each aubergine and stuff two halves of garlic into each. Lay on the grill and cook for 20 minutes, turning occasionally, until the skins are charred all over and the aubergines are starting to collapse. Transfer to a plate or tray and leave to cool.

Cut the aubergines in half lengthways and scoop the flesh out with a spoon, ensuring that you discard any charred pieces of skin. Spoon the flesh into a sieve and gently press down with the back of a spoon to remove as much liquid as possible. Tip the drained flesh onto a chopping board, top with the tahini, lemon juice and half the sumac and season with sea salt. Roughly chop everything together, scraping the mixture into the middle of the board as you go. Once you have a rough paste and all the tahini has been mixed in, have a taste and add a little more salt or lemon juice if needed.

Scoop the aubergine mixture into a serving bowl, sprinkle over the remaining sumac and serve with Flatbreads for dipping.

BLACKENED TOMATO SALSA

I make this salsa whenever I cook Mexican food and love that it can be warm and smoky, while still being really fresh and vibrant. Don't be afraid to burn the tomatoes and chillies; it's that deep charring that gives this salsa its unique, smoky roasted flavour. Also, by roasting the onions you take away that raw edge and intensify their sweetness.

SERVES 4 | PREP TIME: 15 MINUTES | COOK TIME: 10 MINUTES PLUS COOLING

2 red chillies
4 garlic cloves, unpeeled
5 ripe tomatoes
1 red onion, peeled but
   root left intact and cut
   into wedges
juice of 1 lime
pinch of caster sugar
pinch of sea salt flakes
1 small bunch of coriander,
   roughly chopped

You will need one long
   metal skewer.

Preheat the barbecue for direct grilling (see page 11). Thread the chillies and garlic cloves onto the skewer and lay on the grill with the tomatoes and onion. Cook for 5 minutes, turning regularly, until the skins are charred and the tomatoes start to soften. Remove the chillies, garlic and onion from the grill and set aside. Cook the tomatoes for a further 5 minutes, then remove from the grill and leave to cool.

Put the tomatoes into a sieve set over a bowl and roughly mash with the back of the spoon. The aim is to get rid of all the excess liquid but keep all the sweet, smoky flesh and skin. You don't need the juice that collects underneath, but it's delicious, so save it for a sauce or, better still, a Bloody Mary the next morning.

Peel the garlic and remove the stalks and seeds from the chillies. Pile them up on a chopping board with the onion and roughly chop everything together. Add the lime juice, sugar, salt and coriander to the pile and continue to chop. Finally, add the tomatoes, give everything a final chop and mix, then scoop into a serving dish.

TZATZIKI

Once you've made this fresh, garlicky dip, you'll wonder why you ever bought the bland, ready-made stuff. It's ready in a flash, livens up grilled meat and cools down anything fiery.

MAKES APPROX. 350ML | PREP TIME: 5 MINUTES PLUS (PREFERABLY) CHILLING

½ cucumber
1 small garlic clove, crushed
2 tablespoons extra virgin olive
   oil, plus extra for drizzling
250ml thick Greek yogurt
1 small bunch of mint, leaves
   finely chopped
sea salt and freshly ground
   black pepper

Peel and deseed the cucumber, then coarsely grate. Combine the cucumber with the remaining ingredients in a bowl and stir thoroughly, ensuring that the garlic is well mixed in. Season with salt and plenty of black pepper. Spoon into a serving bowl, drizzle with extra olive oil and serve.

The tzatziki is ready to eat straight away, but really benefits from a couple of hours in the fridge, tightly covered with clingfilm, for the flavours to develop.

PICO de GALLO with CHARRED CORN

Pico de gallo is the classic fresh tomato salsa associated with Mexican food. It features fresh tomatoes, crunchy onions, chilli and lime juice, but I've added charred sweetcorn for a bit of smoky sweetness. It's delicious as a side or for dipping tortilla chips while you grill the main event.

SERVES 4 AS A SIDE | PREP TIME: 10 MINUTES | COOK TIME: 10 MINUTES

fine sea salt
2 sweetcorn cobs
6 spring onions, trimmed
4 ripe tomatoes, roughly
  chopped
2 red chillies, finely chopped
1 red onion, finely chopped
1 garlic clove, crushed
1 teaspoon chipotle paste
juice of 1–2 limes
pinch of caster sugar
1 small bunch of coriander,
  roughly chopped
freshly ground black pepper

Preheat the barbecue for direct grilling (see page 11).

Bring a large saucepan of salted water to the boil, add the sweetcorn and cook for 3 minutes, then drain thoroughly.

Lay the sweetcorn and spring onions on the grill and cook for 4–5 minutes until charred and starting to soften, turning occasionally.

Remove from the grill and transfer to a chopping board. When cool enough to handle, roughly chop the spring onions, and run a knife down the length of the corn cobs to remove the kernels. Combine in a serving bowl with the remaining ingredients, season to taste and serve.

SWEET CHILLI SAUCE

I originally wrote this recipe to serve with the Sticky Chilli Pork Belly (page 28), but it goes so well with grilled meat and fish that I had to include it as a recipe in its own right. Good Thai sweet chilli sauces are readily available, but you can't beat homemade.

MAKES APPROX. 600ML | PREP TIME: 10 MINUTES PLUS COOLING | COOK TIME: 25 MINUTES

300g long red chillies,
  stalks removed
3 garlic cloves, peeled
450ml white wine vinegar
350g caster sugar
2 teaspoons fine sea salt

Roughly chop half the chillies and put them in a food processor. Deseed the remaining chillies, ensuring that you remove the membranes (that's where the real heat lies), then roughly chop and add to the food processor along with the garlic cloves. Blend until finely chopped, scraping down the sides of the bowl occasionally to catch any errant large chunks of chilli.

Tip the chilli paste into a large saucepan, stir in the vinegar, sugar and salt and bring to the boil. Boil for 3–4 minutes, stirring occasionally, until the sugar has completely dissolved then reduce the heat to a gentle simmer; the surface of the liquid should only be lightly bubbling. Continue simmering for 20 minutes, scraping any flecks of chilli from the side of the pan as the sauce reduces.

Remove from the heat and leave to cool slightly before pouring into sterilised jars or bottles and sealing. The sauce will keep in the fridge for up to 3 months.

KIMCHI

Every now and again you discover a food or flavour that totally rocks your world and kimchi fits firmly in that category. I was introduced to kimchi, the funky Korean fermented vegetable dish, a few years ago by my colleague and friend Rob, whose mum is Korean. He's a passionate advocate for Korean food and with good reason; it's awesome. The most common type of kimchi is made with cabbage, although there are lots of varieties made from all sorts of vegetables. A good kimchi should have a nice crunch, a deep flavour from chilli, garlic and ginger and that familiar tingle that only comes from being slowly fermented. The Korean chilli powder, kochukaru, is really important so do try to track it down; I've tried standard red chilli powder and it doesn't taste the same.

MAKES 1 LARGE JAR, APPROX. 1.5 LITRES | PREP TIME: 25 MINUTES PLUS FERMENTING

1 Chinese cabbage
3 tablespoons sea salt flakes
12 garlic cloves, roughly
    chopped
50g fresh ginger, peeled
    and roughly chopped
3 tablespoons fish sauce
1 tablespoon caster sugar
5 tablespoons kochukaru
    (Korean red chilli powder)
100ml water
1 daikon
6 fat spring onions, green
    parts cut into 3cm lengths,
    white parts finely sliced
1 large carrot, peeled, halved
    lengthways and finely sliced

Trim the base off the cabbage and separate the cabbage into individual leaves. Wash thoroughly and then chop into roughly 5cm pieces. Tip into a large bowl, sprinkle over the salt and cover tightly with clingfilm. Give the bowl a good shake to ensure that the cabbage is evenly coated in the salt, then chill for 4 hours.

Drain the cabbage and rinse thoroughly in cold water; you'll need to rinse the cabbage at least three times to get rid of the excess salt. If you're not sure, have a nibble – it should taste a little salty but not unbearably so.

Put the garlic, ginger, fish sauce and sugar into a small food processor and blend to a smooth paste. Tip into a large bowl and stir in the chilli powder and water. Peel the daikon, cut it in half lengthways and slice into half-rounds. Add to the chilli paste along with the spring onions, carrot and cabbage. Give everything a good stir to ensure that all the vegetables are nicely coated, then cover with clingfilm and chill for 24 hours.

After 24 hours the kimchi is ready to eat, but will taste far better after a week or so of fermenting. Transfer to a 1.5-litre, sterilised jar, leave in the back of the fridge and be patient. Kimchi lasts for a good few months, but becomes increasingly potent over time; anything over a month old is not for the faint-hearted.

PICKLED GREEN CHILLIES

These are a storecupboard must-have and are as versatile as they are delicious. This works with any chillies, so choose your favourite variety according to how brave/foolhardy you are. I tend to knock up two batches at once; one milder and one fiery.

MAKES 1 LARGE JAR APPROX. 1.5 LITRES │ PREP TIME: 5 MINUTES PLUS COOLING │ COOK TIME: 5 MINUTES

500g green chillies
500ml water
500ml white wine vinegar
2 tablespoons caster sugar
1 tablespoon fine sea salt

Prick each chilli a couple of times with a metal skewer, then pack into a 1.5-litre, sterilised clip-top jar.

Combine the water, vinegar, sugar and salt in a saucepan and bring to the boil. Cook for 2 minutes until the sugar and salt have dissolved, stirring occasionally. Carefully pour onto the chillies, pushing them down to make sure they're all submerged. Give the jar a couple of taps to get rid of any hidden air bubbles, then seal and leave to cool. Put the jar in a cool, dark place and leave for a week. Once opened, store in the fridge for up to 3 months.

VARIATION: For pickled jalapeños, follow the recipe as above using 500g fresh jalapeño chillies. Try to find really firm, dark green jalapeños, as they'll retain their crunch. Use on burgers or as a side for Mexican dishes.

PINK PICKLED ONIONS

These are a great little pickle to go with all sorts of barbecued food and look amazing, as the onions turn an electric pink when they're pickled. During barbecue season I've always got a stash of these in the fridge, ready to add a sweet and sour crunch to salads and kebabs.

MAKES 1 SMALL JAR APPROX. 500ML │PREP TIME: 5 MINUTES PLUS COOLING │COOK TIME: 5 MINUTES

2 red onions, thinly sliced
150ml water
150ml cider vinegar
125g caster sugar
1 teaspoon fine sea salt

Put the onions in a large heatproof bowl. Combine the water, vinegar, sugar and salt in a saucepan and bring to the boil. Cook for 2 minutes until the sugar and salt have dissolved, stirring occasionally. Remove from the heat and pour over the onions.

Leave to cool to room temperature and then drain. They're ready to serve straight away but will keep in an airtight container in the fridge for up to a week.

CHIMICHURRI

Whether they're sharp and spicy to cut through rich dishes or sweet and smoky for dipping and mopping, my barbecue isn't complete without a few of these sauces on the table.

SERVES 6 | PREP TIME: 10 MINUTES PLUS STANDING

2 garlic cloves, crushed
2 red chillies, deseeded
  and finely chopped
2 tablespoons red wine vinegar
2 teaspoons dried oregano
½ teaspoon chilli flakes
100g flat-leaf parsley
olive oil, for mixing
sea salt and freshly ground
  black pepper

Mix together the garlic, chillies, vinegar, oregano and chilli flakes in a large bowl and leave to stand for 10 minutes.

Chop the parsley very finely, add to the bowl and stir in enough olive oil to loosen. Season to taste with sea salt and black pepper.

QUICK SHARP BARBECUE SAUCE

MAKES APPROX. 350ML | COOK TIME: 10 MINUTES PLUS COOLING

150ml cider vinegar
150g tomato ketchup
2 tablespoons Dijon mustard
1 tablespoon Hot Sauce
  (page 128) or Tabasco sauce
1 tablespoon dark soy sauce
1 tablespoon black treacle
1 teaspoon chipotle paste
1 teaspoon sweet smoked
  paprika

Pour the ingredients into a saucepan, bring to a gentle simmer and cook for 5 minutes. Remove from the heat and leave to cool.

Decant into a sterilised bottle, seal and store in the fridge for up to a month.

HOT SAUCE

MAKES APPROX. 600ML | PREP TIME: 5 MINUTES PLUS COOLING | COOK TIME: 20 MINUTES

350g long red chillies
1 garlic bulb, unpeeled
1 ripe tomato, roughly chopped
250ml white wine vinegar
2 teaspoons caster sugar
½ teaspoon fine sea salt
150ml water

Preheat the oven to 220°C/gas mark 7 and line a baking tray with greaseproof paper. Prick the chillies with a small sharp knife and lay on the tray with the garlic bulb. Roast for 20 minutes, shaking the tray halfway through cooking. Leave to cool completely.

Trim away the chilli stalks, peel the garlic and tip into a liquidiser with the remaining ingredients. Blend until smooth and then pour into sterilised bottles and seal. Kept refrigerated the sauce will last up to 3 months and gets better with age.

SMOKY BOURBON SAUCE

MAKES 600ML | PREP TIME: 10 MINUTES PLUS COOLING | COOK TIME: 45 MINUTES

2 tablespoons olive oil
3 onions, thinly sliced
6 chipotle chillies
5 cloves
2 teaspoons cumin seeds
2 teaspoons fennel seeds
1 teaspoon chilli flakes
1 teaspoon freshly ground black
    pepper
1 Hot-smoked Garlic Bulb
    (page 152)
2 tablespoons tomato purée
4 tablespoons dark muscovado
    sugar
500ml apple juice
2 tablespoons Worcestershire
    sauce
250ml cider vinegar
250ml bourbon

Heat the oil in a large, heavy-based saucepan, add the onions and fry gently for 30 minutes, stirring, until soft and caramelised.

Meanwhile, put the chipotle chillies into a small bowl, cover with boiling water and leave to soak for 10 minutes. Drain, leave to cool and then remove the stalks and seeds.

Toast the cloves and cumin and fennel seeds for 2 minutes in a dry frying pan, then grind to a fine powder with the chilli flakes and pepper using a pestle and mortar or a spice grinder.

Once the onions are nice and sticky, add the garlic and chipotle chillies and cook for 2 minutes. Add the spice mix and fry for a minute, then add the tomato purée and sugar and fry for 2 minutes. Add the apple juice and Worcestershire sauce and bring to the boil, then reduce the heat and simmer for 5 minutes. Finally, pour in the vinegar and bourbon and simmer for a further 5 minutes to burn off the alcohol.

Remove from the heat and leave to cool, then pour into a liquidiser and blend until smooth. Pass through a fine-meshed sieve into a jug, pour into sterilised jars and seal. This tastes delicious straight away, but the flavour really develops over time. Kept refrigerated it'll last up to 3 months.

SALSA VERDE

Perfect with grilled fish, meat or vegetables, this classic Italian sauce should be made as last minute as possible to keep it vibrant and fresh. Don't be tempted to cheat and use a food processor, as it will bruise the herbs and you'll get a dull, watery sauce.

SERVES 6 | PREP TIME: 10 MINUTES

100g flat-leaf parsley
50g mint leaves
50g basil leaves
olive oil, for mixing
2 tablespoons capers
4 anchovy fillets, drained
1 fat garlic clove, crushed
2 tablespoons red wine vinegar
1 tablespoon Dijon mustard
sea salt and freshly ground
    black pepper

Pile the herbs up on a chopping board and roughly chop, adding a little olive oil as you go to keep everything fresh and green. Add the capers, anchovies and garlic and chop finely. Scrape into a bowl and stir in the vinegar, mustard and enough olive oil to loosen, then season to taste with salt and pepper.

Salsa verde should always be made fresh and is best eaten straight away, but any left over will keep in the fridge, tightly covered with clingfilm, for a day and is great for livening up some simple boiled potatoes or grilled vegetables.

MAYONNAISE

You can't beat making your own mayonnaise. Make sure that you have a steady hand and begin by adding the oil very, very slowly. If the mixture splits, start again with fresh yolks, then gradually whisk the split mixture into the new batch.

MAKES 300ML | PREP TIME: 10 MINUTES

2 medium egg yolks
1 garlic clove,
    crushed (optional)
1 teaspoon Dijon mustard
fine sea salt
200ml vegetable oil
50ml extra virgin
    rapeseed oil
squeeze of lemon juice,
    to taste

Put the egg yolks, garlic and mustard into a large bowl, add a good pinch of salt and whisk together until smooth. Combine the oils in a jug and, whisking constantly, begin to pour the oil into the bowl in a very thin, steady stream. It's crucial that you really take your time at this stage; overzealous oil pouring will lead to a split mayonnaise. Continue steadily adding the oil and whisking until it's all incorporated.

Whisk in lemon juice to taste and add a pinch more salt if needed. At this stage you can add any additional flavourings, such as chopped herbs, smoked paprika or roasted garlic.

BÉARNAISE SAUCE

This classic sauce needs to be rich and creamy from the egg yolks and plenty of butter, with a background acidity from the vinegar and that familiar aniseed flavour from the tarragon. If you're grilling steak or chicken, this needs to be served alongside.

SERVES 6 | PREP TIME: 10 MINUTES | COOK TIME: 25 MINUTES

250g unsalted butter
1 small bunch of tarragon,
    stalks and leaves separated
1 large shallot, roughly
    chopped
100ml dry white wine
2 tablespoons white
    wine vinegar
½ teaspoon white
    peppercorns
1 bay leaf, torn in half
3 medium egg yolks
sea salt and ground
    white pepper

Put the butter in a small saucepan and set over the lowest heat. Once the butter has melted, slowly pour the clear yellow liquid into a jug, leaving behind the white milk solids.

Put the tarragon stalks, shallot, wine, vinegar, peppercorns and bay leaf into a small saucepan, bring to the boil and cook until reduced to about 50ml. Strain the liquid into a large, heatproof bowl and whisk in the egg yolks.

Set the bowl over a pan of simmering water and whisk the egg yolk mixture. Continue whisking for 3–4 minutes until the mixture begins to thicken, then start to whisk in the clarified butter in a very slow, steady stream. Once all the butter has been incorporated, remove the bowl from the heat and season to taste. Finely chop the tarragon leaves and stir into the sauce.

This sauce is perfect as it is, but if you're cooking steaks and want to make it 'dirty', whisk in the resting juices from the steaks. It's not exactly traditional, but seriously tasty.

SMOKING

BRISKET

Brisket perfectly demonstrates the brilliance of cooking low and slow over gently smouldering charcoal and wood. It's a tough, hard-working slab of meat that needs a lot of time and love to bring out the flavour. Relatively basic – just a large piece of good-quality beef, seasoned with the simplest of dry rubs – done well, brisket tastes extraordinary. I've kept my recipe straightforward to give you more of a beginner's guide on how to cook it. There are lots of variables – the type and size of barbecue you own, the fat to meat ratio, the thickness of the meat and so on – so it's as much about using your instinct as following a recipe. A digital probe thermometer is a useful piece of kit if you're not feeling too confident or simply want a bit of help the first time you try it.

SERVES 8–10 | PREP TIME: 15 MINUTES | COOK TIME: 9–10 HOURS PLUS RESTING

4.5kg beef brisket joint
3 tablespoons coarsely
  ground black pepper
3 tablespoons fine sea salt

Remove the brisket from the fridge at least 2 hours before cooking. Preheat the barbecue or smoker for indirect grilling (see page 11). Lay the brisket in an old large roasting tray. Combine the salt and pepper in a small bowl and scatter over the brisket in an even layer. It's really important to achieve an even coating and that can be quite tricky to do, so I now save any old salt containers – the type with the different hole sizes on a wheel on top – to fill with the seasoning mix and shake over the meat, patting it into the surface as I go.

Remove the brisket from the tray, lay on the grill fat-side up and insert a digital probe thermometer into the thickest part of the meat. Close the lid and cook for 5 hours until the brisket has a rich, dark bark all over.

Carefully remove the brisket from the barbecue or smoker and wrap in foil (you'll need to wear oven gloves to handle the brisket and you may need some help with this). Return to the barbecue or smoker and continue cooking for a further 4–5 hours or until the internal temperature hits 86–88°C.

Remove the brisket from the barbecue or smoker and set aside to rest for 30 minutes before unwrapping and slicing.

SMOKED CHICKEN

This is a great alternative to roast chicken and so simple to prepare. The low, slow smoking means that you won't get lovely crispy skin, but that is made up for with beautifully moist, lightly smoked meat. As the chicken rests the juices collect to make a delicious smoked meaty jelly; I mix this with the shredded chicken or save it to enrich gravy or sauces. A digital probe thermometer is handy to ensure that the chicken is cooked through, while keeping the meat really moist.

SERVES 6 | PREP TIME: 10 MINUTES | COOK TIME: 2–2½ HOURS PLUS RESTING

1 free-range chicken,
    weighing approx. 1.8kg
1 tablespoon fine sea salt
2 teaspoons coarsely
    ground black pepper
2 teaspoons paprika
1 teaspoon dried thyme

Preheat the barbecue or smoker for indirect grilling (see page 11). Lay the chicken in a foil tray or an old roasting tray and pat dry with kitchen paper. Combine the salt, pepper, paprika and thyme in a small bowl, then rub over the surface of the chicken, using any leftover rub to season inside the cavity.

Insert a digital probe thermometer into the thickest part of the thigh and set the tray on the grill. Close the lid and smoke for 2–2½ hours or until the internal temperature reads 70°C.

Remove the chicken from the barbecue or smoker and leave to rest for 20 minutes, then carve or, as I prefer, tear the meat into chunks and serve.

LAMB SHAWARMA

This dish takes hardly any time to prepare, so you can leave it to cook away for hours with little fuss and the pay-off is sweet, wonderfully tender meat heady with fragrant spices. A great sharing dish; just tear the lamb into pieces and serve with the onion salad and a whole host of condiments, then let everyone dive in and build their own.

SERVES 6 | PREP TIME: 20 MINUTES PLUS MARINATING | COOK TIME: 6–7 HOURS PLUS RESTING

2kg shoulder of lamb
  on the bone

FOR THE MARINADE
3 garlic cloves, crushed
30g fresh ginger, peeled
  and chopped
juice of 1 lemon
50ml olive oil
2 teaspoons dark brown
  soft sugar
2 teaspoons fine sea salt
2 tablespoons ras el hanout
1 teaspoon ground cinnamon

FOR THE ONION SALAD
1 large sweet white onion,
  finely chopped
1 garlic clove, finely chopped
1 small bunch of parsley,
  finely chopped
1 small bunch of coriander,
  finely chopped
2 teaspoons red wine vinegar
sea salt and freshly ground
  black pepper

TO SERVE
warm Flatbreads (page 117)
  or pitta breads
Hot Sauce (page 128)
Pickled Green Chillies (page 126)
tahini
2 Lebanese cucumbers, sliced
2 ripe tomatoes, sliced

Lay the lamb in a large roasting tray. Blend the marinade ingredients together in a food processor until smooth, pour over the lamb and massage into the meat. Cover with clingfilm and marinate in the fridge for at least 4 hours; overnight is preferable.

Remove the lamb from the fridge an hour before cooking. Preheat the barbecue for indirect grilling (see page 11). Lay the lamb on the grill, close the lid and cook for 3 hours.

Remove the lamb from the grill and wrap in foil, then return it to the grill for a further 3–4 hours until deliciously tender. The best way to check if the lamb is cooked is to take hold of the shoulder blade, which will be nicely protruding by now, and give it a gentle twist. If it moves easily and feels like you could pull it out cleanly, the lamb is ready. Set it aside to rest for 30 minutes.

Meanwhile, combine the ingredients for the onion salad in a bowl and season to taste.

To serve, pull the bone out of the lamb, then carefully pull the meat apart into chunky strands; ensure that you don't shred it too finely or you'll lose the texture. Pile the lamb into warm Flatbreads, top with the onion salad and serve with Hot Sauce, Pickled Green Chillies, tahini and the sliced cucumbers and tomatoes.

SMOKED TOMATOES
with **LARDO** di **COLONNATA**

I first tried this in Urbino, Italy, where everything was cooked in a wood-fired oven. Lardo is a fantastic ingredient and really makes this dish; it's cured pork back fat, which gently melts with the heat of the tomatoes, transforming a simple warm salad into something rich and utterly delicious. Track down the lardo – from a good Italian deli or online suppliers – it's worth it.

SERVES 6–8 AS A SIDE DISH | **PREP TIME: 10 MINUTES** | **COOK TIME: 2½ HOURS**

1kg plum tomatoes, halved
3 garlic cloves, crushed
4 sprigs of rosemary,
    leaves chopped
3 tablespoons extra
    virgin olive oil
sea salt and freshly
    ground black pepper
50g lardo, finely diced

Preheat the barbecue or smoker for indirect grilling (see page 11). Lay the tomatoes cut-side up on a roasting tray. Mix the garlic and rosemary with the oil, brush over the tomatoes and season. Set the tray on the grill, close the lid and smoke for 2 hours until the tomatoes have softened and wrinkled.

Top each tomato with a few pieces of lardo and cook for a further 30 minutes until the lard begins to melt.

Arrange the smoked tomatoes on a platter and serve.

PORK LOIN with PICKLED APPLES

Somewhere between roast pork and smoked ham, this is just as tasty cold as it is hot. A digital probe thermometer is useful; as pork loin is very lean, it can dry out easily, but cooked to precisely the right temperature, it stays beautifully moist.

SERVES 6 | PREP TIME: 15 MINUTES | COOK TIME: 1 HOUR PLUS RESTING

2kg pork loin joint, trimmed of all excess fat and sinew

FOR THE RUB
1 tablespoon fine sea salt
2 teaspoons cracked black pepper
2 teaspoons dark brown soft sugar
1 teaspoon paprika
1 teaspoon onion granules

FOR THE PICKLED APPLES
100g caster sugar
150ml cider vinegar
150ml water
1 teaspoon fine sea salt
2 Granny Smith apples
2 Braeburn apples

You will need a large handful of wood chips (see page 12), soaked in warm water for 30 minutes.

Remove the pork from the fridge an hour before cooking and preheat the barbecue or smoker for indirect grilling (see page 11) and add the soaked wood chips.

Combine the rub ingredients in a small bowl, place the pork in a large tray to catch any excess and then rub evenly into the meat. Lift the pork out of the tray and lay on the grill, close the lid and smoke for 1 hour, topping up the wood chips as needed. Turn the pork roughly halfway through cooking and insert a digital probe thermometer into the thickest part. When the pork reaches 65°C, remove from the grill, wrap tightly in a double layer of foil and leave to rest for 20 minutes.

While the pork is smoking, prepare the apples. Bring the sugar, vinegar, water and salt to the boil in a small saucepan and simmer until the sugar has completely dissolved. Remove from the heat and leave to cool slightly. Core, halve and thinly slice the apples, adding them to the vinegar mixture as you go to prevent them from discolouring. Leave to stand for 30 minutes, then cover and chill in the fridge for 30 minutes before draining.

Thinly slice the pork and serve with the pickled apples and a simple salad.

VARIATION: For a more substantial snack, serve in a brioche roll spread with Dijon mustard.

PULLED PORK

Proper pulled pork relies on very little additional flavour, just a simple dry rub and a long, slow cook over gently smouldering wood and charcoal. I often smoke mine overnight so that I'm less tempted to poke and prod at it and less likely to get into trouble with the neighbours (smoking meat doesn't go down well when people have washing hanging out to dry!). Ask your butcher for a half shoulder of pork with the skin, chine bone and any rib bones removed. You should be left with a large piece of pork with a decent layer of fat on the outside and a single shoulder blade bone running through the middle.

SERVES 6–8 | PREP TIME: 5 MINUTES | COOK TIME: 6–7 HOURS PLUS RESTING

3kg prepared (see recipe introduction) half shoulder of pork

FOR THE DRY RUB
2 tablespoons cracked black pepper
1 tablespoon fine sea salt
1 tablespoon demerara sugar
1 tablespoon paprika

TO SERVE
brioche rolls or Potato Rolls (page 115)
Chipotle Slaw (page 101)
Smoky Bourbon Sauce (page 129)

Remove the pork from the fridge an hour before cooking and preheat the barbecue or smoker for indirect grilling (see page 11). Put the rub ingredients in a mortar and grind to a fine powder with a pestle. Lay the pork bone-side down in an old large roasting tray and coat evenly in the rub. Set the tray on the grill, close the lid and cook for 4 hours or until the pork has a deep mahogany-coloured bark.

Remove the pork from the barbecue or smoker and wrap tightly in foil, then return to the barbecue or smoker and cook for 2–3 hours until it reaches an internal temperature of 90°C. Remove and leave to rest, wrapped in the foil, for 30 minutes.

Unwrap the pork and pour the resting juices into a large bowl. Wearing disposable gloves, or using two forks, carefully pull the meat into thick strands, discarding the large pieces of fat and the bone as you go. Toss the meat in the resting juices and serve in brioche rolls or Potato Rolls with Chipotle Slaw and Smoky Bourbon Sauce.

SMOKED BONE MARROW
on TOAST

Bone marrow is totally underrated. If you've never tried it, imagine the most delicious, beefy butter gently melting into lightly charred sourdough toast. Now imagine it slightly smoked. If you're starting to salivate, then try this recipe.

SERVES 4 AS A STARTER OR SNACK | PREP TIME: 5 MINUTES | COOK TIME: 35 MINUTES

4 pieces of bone marrow, 15cm in length, halved lengthways
fine sea salt and freshly ground black pepper
4 thick slices of sourdough bread
1 garlic clove, peeled
sherry vinegar, for drizzling
1 small bunch of flat-leaf parsley, finely chopped

You will need a handful of wood chips (see page 12), soaked in warm water for 30 minutes.

Preheat the barbecue or smoker for indirect grilling (see page 11) and add the soaked wood chips. Season the bone marrow pieces and lay cut-side up in a foil tray or an old roasting tray. Set the tray on the grill, close the lid and smoke for 30 minutes, then remove from the grill and cover with foil.

Get the barbecue or smoker ready for direct grilling (see page 11). Lay the bread on the grill and toast for a few minutes until crisp and lightly charred, turning regularly, then rub with the garlic clove. Spoon the soft bone marrow over the toast, drizzle with a little sherry vinegar and scatter over the parsley. Season with a little more salt and pepper before serving.

SMOKED CHICKEN SALAD
with **BUTTERMILK DRESSING**

Hot smoking doesn't have to be all about huge slabs of meat. Simple chicken breasts can be totally transformed by cooking them low over smouldering charcoal and wood, and they stay really moist and tender. But this salad is as much about the dressing as it is about the chicken. It has a richness from the Parmesan but also a lovely sharpness from the buttermilk and lemon juice, which cuts through the smoky chicken perfectly.

SERVES 4 | **PREP TIME: 15 MINUTES** | **COOK TIME: 20 MINUTES**

1 teaspoon fine sea salt
1 teaspoon coarsely ground
  black pepper
4 free-range skinless,
  boneless chicken breasts

FOR THE DRESSING
150ml buttermilk
2 tablespoons olive oil
25g Parmesan cheese,
  finely grated
juice of ½ lemon
1 garlic clove, crushed
2 tablespoons finely
  chopped chives
sea salt and freshly ground
  black pepper

FOR THE SALAD
2 slices of white
  sourdough bread
olive oil, for brushing
2 heads of romaine lettuce,
  leaves separated, washed
  and dried, then torn
500g mixed tomatoes, sliced
1 large bunch of breakfast
  radishes, trimmed and
  halved lengthways

You will need a large handful
of wood chips (see page 12),
soaked in warm water for
30 minutes.

Preheat the barbecue or smoker for indirect grilling (see page 11) and add the soaked wood chips. Combine the salt and pepper in a small bowl, then sprinkle over the chicken in an even layer, ensuring that the meat is evenly covered. Lay the chicken breasts on the grill, close the lid and smoke for 20 minutes or until the chicken is cooked through.

Meanwhile, combine the dressing ingredients except the chives and seasoning in a jug and blend with a stick blender until emulsified (you could also do this in a liquidiser). Stir in the chives and season to taste.

Once the chicken is cooked, remove it from the grill and wrap it in foil. Get the barbecue or smoker ready for direct grilling (see page 11), lightly brush the bread on each side with olive oil and lay on the grill. Toast the bread for a few minutes until crisp and lightly charred, turning regularly. Leave to cool for a minute, then tear into bite-sized pieces. Put the toast, lettuce, tomatoes and radishes into a large bowl, pour over the dressing and toss to coat. Tip the salad onto a large platter, then thickly slice the chicken and arrange on top.

HAY-SMOKED LAMB
with WHITE ONION PURÉE

I love working on live TV shows; it's a fast-paced, busy environment which can be highly stressful but also gets the adrenaline going and can be a lot of fun. This recipe is an adaptation of a dish cooked by the magnificently talented Scottish chef Tom Kitchin. He came on a live Saturday morning show that I was working on and cooked a beautiful rack of lamb smoked in hay. However, as we rehearsed, we created so much smoke it set off the fire alarms and the studio had to be evacuated! The smouldering hay in this recipe gives the lamb a delicate, sweet smoked flavour. The best place to get hold of the hay is a pet shop; ask for the stuff used for animal feed (rather than bedding hay), as it'll have been washed.

SERVES 4 | PREP TIME: 15 MINUTES | COOK TIME: 45 MINUTES

4 lamb rumps
fine sea salt

FOR THE WHITE ONION PURÉE
25g unsalted butter
splash of olive oil
4 sweet white onions, finely sliced
2 garlic cloves, crushed
pinch of fine sea salt
100ml double cream
ground white pepper

Salsa Verde (page 129), to serve

You will need 2 large handfuls of hay.

First make the onion purée. Melt the butter in a heavy-based pan with the oil and add the onions and garlic along with the salt, which will draw the moisture from the onions and stop them taking on any colour as they cook. Cook gently for 15 minutes until the onions are really soft, stirring often. Close the lid and cook for a further 15 minutes. Stir in the cream and season with white pepper, then pour everything into a liquidiser and blend until really smooth. Transfer to a clean pan, cover and set aside.

Remove the lamb rumps from the fridge 30 minutes before cooking and preheat the barbecue for direct grilling (see page 11). Lightly score the fat on the lamb rumps and season with salt. Lay on the grill and cook for 3–4 minutes until golden brown, turning regularly. Remove from the heat; I tend to lift the whole grill off at this point to make things easier.

Wet the hay by quickly flashing it under a running tap; it needs to be slightly damp rather than soaked. Throw the hay onto the coals, then put the grill and the lamb back on top, close the lid and open the top and bottom vents. The smoke will start to billow out, but don't worry, it's meant to. Cook for 10 minutes, then remove the lamb and set aside to rest for 5 minutes.

While the lamb rests, gently reheat the onion purée. Slice the lamb and serve with the purée and Salsa Verde.

SMOKED TIGER PRAWNS
with DIRTY ROMESCO SAUCE

Sweet, nutty Romesco is such a full-bodied sauce that whatever you serve with it really needs to be kept simple. My version is cooked 'dirty', which simply means that the pepper and tomatoes are cooked straight on the coals, giving a great smoky edge. I love it spooned onto hot toast, or served alongside grilled vegetables for dipping, but its true calling has to be as a partner for seafood. I smoke the prawns with the shell on to protect the sweet flesh from drying out or taking on too much smoke, but also to impart loads of flavour.

SERVES 4 | PREP TIME: 15 MINUTES PLUS SOAKING | COOK TIME: 15 MINUTES

24 large raw tiger prawns,
　　shell on
fine sea salt

FOR THE ROMESCO SAUCE
2 dried Spanish ñora
　　peppers, deseeded
1 red pepper
2 ripe tomatoes
50g toasted flaked almonds
1 garlic clove, crushed
2 tablespoons extra virgin
　　olive oil
1 slice of white bread, crusts
　　removed, torn into chunks
sea salt flakes
sherry vinegar, to taste

crusty bread, to serve

You will need a large handful of wood chips (see page 12), soaked in warm water for 30 minutes.

Soak the dried peppers in boiling water for 1 hour, then drain. Preheat the barbecue or smoker for indirect grilling (see page 11) and add the soaked wood chips. While the charcoal is still glowing white, lay the red pepper and tomatoes directly on the coals and cook for 5 minutes, turning occasionally, until the pepper is blackened all over and the tomatoes are blistered and softened. Remove from the coals and leave to cool.

Carefully rub away all the charred exterior from the pepper; the skin will come away and you'll be left with sweet, smoky flesh. Don't be tempted to rinse it, as you'll wash away all the flavour. Discard the stalk and seeds.

Get rid of any particularly charred bits of tomato skin, then roughly chop. Put the almonds, garlic and oil into a food processor and blend until smooth. Add the bread and blend to a rough paste, then season to taste with salt and the vinegar.

When the charcoal has died down, add the wood chips and allow the smoke to build up before laying the prawns on the grill in an even layer and sprinkling over a little salt. Close the lid and smoke for 10–12 minutes until cooked through.

Serve the prawns with the Romesco sauce and crusty bread.

SMOKED ONIONS
with THYME BUTTER

This is one of my easiest recipes, and it came about when I was smoking a shoulder of pork and had a couple of spare onions, so I threw them in alongside to see what would happen. The result was soft, sweet roast onions with a subtle smoked flavour. They make a great side dish to simple grilled meat. Ensure that you pierce the skins to allow the smoke to penetrate the onions and stop them from splitting open during cooking.

SERVES 4 AS A SIDE | PREP TIME: 5 MINUTES | COOK TIME: 3 HOURS

4 onions, unpeeled
6 sprigs of thyme,
    leaves picked
good pinch of sea
    salt flakes
50g unsalted butter,
    at room temperature

Preheat the barbecue or smoker for indirect grilling (see page 11). Take a large sheet of foil and roughly scrunch it up to make a bed for the onions to sit on. Pierce each onion several times with a small, sharp knife. Lay the foil on the grill and sit the onions root down on top. Close the lid and smoke for 3 hours. To check that the onions are cooked, insert the small sharp knife, which should glide straight through with no resistance.

Meanwhile, put the thyme leaves into a mortar with the salt and grind to a fine paste with a pestle. Gradually work the butter in until you have a vibrant green paste. Spoon into a bowl, cover with clingfilm and chill until needed.

I like to serve the onions whole and let everyone unwrap their own and spread with the thyme butter. But if you want to serve them as a platter instead, peel away the outer skins, quarter the onions and dot the butter over the top.

If you happen to have any of the thyme butter left over, and you happen to have some warm, crusty bread... you know what to do.

HOT-SMOKED GARLIC

Smoked garlic is so easy to make and it's far more satisfying than buying it. It adds a lovely subtle smoked flavour to all sort of garlicky treats. I always smoke four or five bulbs at a time, as it keeps well in the fridge (in a sealed container). It's not really worth firing up the barbecue just for a few bulbs of garlic, so chuck them in alongside Brisket (page 134) or Pulled Pork (page 142).

MAKES 4–5 BULBS | PREP TIME: 5 MINUTES | COOK TIME: 3 HOURS

4–5 garlic bulbs

Carefully rub away the papery outer skin from the garlic bulbs; you should be left with a full bulb with all its cloves intact and unpeeled. This way the smoke will penetrate the garlic more easily, but it will still hold together and you won't be fishing cloves out from the coals.

Preheat the barbecue or smoker for indirect grilling (see page 11). Sit the garlic root down on the grill, close the lid and cook for 3 hours until the garlic has taken on a deep brown colour. Remove from the grill and set aside to cool.

SMOKED SEA SALT

If you're smoking a large piece of meat, or have enough glowing embers left at the end of a barbecue, try hot smoking sea salt. It adds a subtle smoky finish to food, and the variation in the end result, which depends on which type of wood you use, is quite distinct.

MAKES 100G | PREP TIME: 5 MINUTES | COOK TIME: 2 HOURS

100g sea salt flakes

You will need a large handful of wood chips (see page 12), soaked in warm water for 30 minutes.

You can smoke the salt as much or as little as you like. Just make an open foil parcel (or use a small foil tray) large enough to hold the salt in a thin, even layer, then add the salt and spread it out.

Preheat the barbecue or smoker for indirect grilling (see page 11) and add the soaked wood chips. Lay the parcel or tray on the grill, close the lid and smoke for 1 hour until the salt has started to take on a deep brown colour.

Remove the parcel or tray from the barbecue or smoker and leave to cool for a couple of minutes. Break the salt up and give it a mix. Return it to the barbecue or smoker for a further hour, then set aside to cool. Store in an airtight container and use in place of regular salt flakes.

SMOKED SALMON

Preparing your own smoked salmon is surprisingly straightforward. You don't need to spend a fortune on equipment – a bit of fridge space, a simple cold smoke generator (see page 12) and a kettle barbecue are sufficient. This recipe is for smoked salmon made with a simple sugar-salt cure, so it's a great starting point if you've never tried cold smoking before. Once you're familiar with the technique, try using different woods for smoking (see page 12); each has its own unique flavour.

SERVES 8–10 | PREP TIME: 15 MINUTES PLUS CURING AND CHILLING | COOK TIME: 10 HOURS

1.8kg side of salmon, skin on, pin bones removed
50g demerara sugar
200g fine sea salt

You will need some smoking wood dust (see page 12); oak or maple work nicely

Lay several sheets of clingfilm on a work surface to make a rectangle roughly three times the width of the salmon and one and a half times the length. Place the salmon on top. Combine the sugar and salt and apply all over the salmon in an even layer. Wrap the salmon tightly in the clingfilm and lay in a tray large enough to catch any liquid that may escape. Place in the fridge for 12 hours.

Unwrap the salmon and rinse off the cure under cold running water. Pat as dry as possible with plenty of kitchen paper and lay flesh-side up on a wire rack. Return to the fridge, uncovered, to dry out for 2 hours, by which time the flesh should feel firm and tacky; it's this sticky surface that will allow the smoke to bond to the outside of the fish.

Set up the barbecue or smoker for cold smoking (see page 12) and add the wood dust. Lay the salmon inside (or hang from a hook if you have one). Smoke for 10 hours. Wrap the salmon in greaseproof paper and chill for a couple of hours before slicing.

SMOKED HERRINGS

Some of my family live on the beautiful Isle of Man which, amongst other things, is famous for its kippered herrings. I've always loved these iconic smoked herrings simply grilled with plenty of butter. Yes, they're a bit bony, but the small amount of effort required to prise away the soft, smoky flesh is worth it. Make sure you use really fresh herrings, as the brining and smoking process relies on the fish being nice and firm.

SERVES 4 | PREP TIME: 20 MINUTES PLUS BRINING AND CHILLING | COOK TIME: 6 HOURS

4 very fresh herrings, weighing approx. 400g each, gutted, scaled and left whole
266g fine sea salt (see note)
1 litre water

TO SERVE
butter
brown toast

You will need some smoking oak dust (see page 12).

First prepare the fish. Insert a sharp knife at the back of the head and cut straight through to the mouth. Then turn the knife around and, keeping it pressed against the spine, cut along the length of the fish through to the tail. You should be left with a herring split open but with the belly intact so that it lays completely flat when opened out. Rinse under cold running water to get rid of any remaining guts and stray scales, then lay in a large, deep tray. Combine the salt and water in a large jug or bowl and stir until the salt has completely dissolved, then pour over the fish. Transfer to the fridge for 20 minutes.

Remove the herring from the brine and rinse under cold running water. Pat dry with plenty of kitchen paper, then lay on a wire rack and return to the fridge, uncovered, for a couple of hours; this will help to dry the fish ready for smoking.

Set up the barbecue or smoker for cold smoking (see page 12). Lay the herrings skin-side down on the grill, close the lid and smoke for 6 hours. Once the herrings are ready, transfer them to the fridge for an hour; at this stage they'll keep there for up to 3 days. Remember, the herrings are smoked but still uncooked, so you'll need to cook them before eating. You can either get the barbecue or smoker ready for direct grilling (see page 11) and lightly grill them for a couple of minutes on each side or poach them in a large pan of simmering water for 5 minutes. Serve with a knob of butter and some hot brown toast.

NOTE: The brine for herrings needs to be made to 80-degree saturation, which is strong enough for the salt solution to penetrate the oily flesh of the herring (hence the very specific amount of salt above). Brining is a more efficient and gentler way of curing, so it's particularly good for herring, which can be quite delicate. As well as helping the smoke adhere to the fish, the brine helps to retain moisture, keeping the herrings really juicy.

SMOKED BUTTER

This works brilliantly wherever you'd normally add a little butter: on top of waxy steamed potatoes, dotted over a steak or whisked into sauces. The great thing about smoking any kind of fat (be it butter, oil or even soured cream) is that it's cheap to prepare and takes on the flavour of smoke relatively quickly, making it perfect for experimenting with. I tend to use a milder smoke – something like beech or maple – but have a play with different woods.

MAKES 250G | COOK TIME: 1 HOUR PLUS CHILLING

250g salted butter,
  cut into 2cm cubes
2 handfuls of ice

You will need some smoking wood dust (see page 12).

Set up the barbecue or smoker for cold smoking (see page 12). Spread the butter out in an even layer in a small foil tray or roasting tray. Stand the tray in a larger foil tray or roasting tray, then half-fill the outer tray with cold water and the ice. Set the two trays on the grill, close the lid and smoke for an hour.

Lift the butter tray out of the water bath and wipe the bottom dry; the water can be quite acrid, so you don't want any of it dripping into the butter. Scrape the butter into a large bowl and beat with a whisk until smooth; the smoke adheres to the surface of the butter, so make sure it's well mixed. Shape into a block or cylinder, wrap in clingfilm and chill for an hour before using.

SMOKED CHEDDAR

I'm a massive cheese fan and love some of the smoked varieties you can buy, so wanted to try smoking my own. Smoking cheese is simple because it doesn't need to be cured, so chuck a block of your favourite Cheddar into a chilled tray and cold smoke it for an hour.

MAKES 250G | COOK TIME: 1 HOUR PLUS CHILLING

250g piece of extra-mature
  Cheddar cheese
2 handfuls of ice

You will need some smoking wood dust (see page 12).

Set up the barbecue or smoker up for cold smoking (see page 12). Lay the piece of cheese in a small foil tray or roasting tray. Stand the tray in a larger foil tray or roasting tray, then half-fill the outer tray with cold water and the ice. Set the two trays on the grill, close the lid and smoke for an hour.

Pat the cheese dry with kitchen paper, wrap in greaseproof paper and chill in the fridge for an hour before using.

COCKTAILS
& COOLERS

MARGARITA de TORONJA PICANTE

My favourite restaurant in Brooklyn is an incredible Mexican place called Gran Eléctrica. Their whole ethos embodies everything that's great about dining out in New York; they take their food seriously, using incredible market produce to create traditional Mexican street food dishes. Naturally, their cocktails are largely designed around tequila, and these two margaritas were so good that I'd happily go back just for them.

MAKES 1 | PREP TIME: 5 MINUTES PLUS INFUSING | COOK TIME: 5 MINUTES PLUS COOLING

45ml Habañero-infused
   Blanco Tequila (see recipe)
15ml triple sec
30ml fresh lime juice
30ml fresh pink
   grapefruit juice
15ml Jalapeño Syrup
   (see recipe)
3–4 ice cubes

FOR THE RIM
grapefruit salt (grapefruit
   zest/sea salt flakes)

GARNISH
½ grapefruit slice

Combine the ingredients in cocktail shaker and shake vigorously. Rub the rim of a rocks glass with grapefruit salt, add 3–4 large solid ice cubes, strain over the cocktail and garnish with a grapefruit slice.

Habañero-infused Blanco Tequila:
Simply quarter 1 habañero chilli and put it in the tequila of choice to infuse. Habañeros can vary in their heat level, so more can be added if necessary but I suggest starting with one.

Jalapeño Syrup (makes approx. 200ml):
In a medium saucepan over a medium heat, combine 125g caster sugar and 125ml water until the sugar dissolves. Add 1 halved, deseeded jalapeño and leave to sit overnight. Strain and refrigerate for up to a month until you're ready to use.

MARGARITA de REMOLACHA

MAKES 1 | PREP TIME: 5 MINUTES | COOK TIME: 5 MINUTES PLUS COOLING

45ml 100% Blue Agave
   Blanco Tequila
15ml triple sec
30ml fresh lime juice
30ml fresh beetroot juice
15ml Simple Syrup (see recipe)
3–4 ice cubes

FOR THE RIM
lime salt (lime zest/sea
   salt flakes)

TO GARNISH
lime wheel
beetroot, sliced thinly

Combine the ingredients in cocktail shaker and shake vigorously. Rub the rim of a rocks glass with lime salt, add 3–4 large solid ice cubes, strain over the cocktail and garnish with a lime wheel and a beetroot slice.

Simple Syrup (makes approx. 200ml):
In a medium saucepan over medium heat, combine 125g caster sugar and 125ml water until the sugar dissolves. Set aside to cool. Once cooled, this will keep for up to month stored in the fridge.

CORN 'N' OIL

I first tried this in Barbados and kicked myself for not bringing home with me a bottle of Velvet Falernum, a sugarcane-based liqueur. You can buy it online and its lightly spiced, citrus flavour really makes this drink. The 'oil' refers to the Bajan blackstrap rum that's traditionally used, but you can use any decent dark rum.

MAKES 1 | PREP TIME: 5 MINUTES

large ice cubes
60ml dark rum
15ml Velvet Falernum
15ml fresh lime juice
4 dashes Angostura bitters
lime wedge, to garnish

Fill a rocks glass with large ice cubes, pour over the remaining ingredients and stir to combine. Garnish with a lime wedge.

DAIQUIRI

A true daiquiri is a crisp, refreshing drink with an addictive sour edge. Because acidity varies from lime to lime, it's important to taste as you go.

MAKES 1 | PREP TIME: 5 MINUTES

ice
60ml silver rum
25ml fresh lime juice
2 teaspoons white caster sugar
lime wheel, to garnish

Fill a cocktail shaker with a mixture of crushed and cubed ice, add the remaining ingredients and shake well. Strain into a chilled coupe glass and garnish with a lime wheel.

RUM PUNCH

'One of sour, two of sweet, three of strong, four of weak.' As long as you remember this rhyme, you'll be able to knock up a perfect rum punch with your eyes closed.

MAKES 1 | PREP TIME: 5 MINUTES

1 part fresh lime juice (20ml)
2 parts mango juice (40ml)
3 parts golden rum (60ml)
4 parts water (80ml)
1 dash Angostura bitters
ice

TO GARNISH
pinch of ground nutmeg
2 maraschino cherries

Combine the ingredients, except the nutmeg and cherries, in a mixing glass or jug filled with ice. Stir to combine then strain into a collins glass filled with ice. Garnish with the nutmeg and cherries and serve.

OLD SMOKY

This recipe is a playful twist born from having the ingredients to hand along with a few glowing coals. It's familiar, but with a hint of smoky burnt sugar. Use the largest ice cubes you can; this is a drink to be sipped slowly, so small ice cubes will water it down as they melt.

MAKES 1 | PREP TIME: 10 MINUTES | COOK TIME: 5 MINUTES

1 piece orange peel
2 large ice cubes
45ml bourbon
15ml smoky single malt whisky
1 teaspoon Charcoal Syrup
  (see below)
4 dashes smoked chilli bitters
1 maraschino cherry, to garnish

FOR THE CHARCOAL SYRUP
100g demerara sugar
100ml water
1 piece of burning-hot charcoal

First make the syrup. Heat the sugar and water in a small saucepan, stirring until the sugar has completely dissolved. Remove from the heat, drop in the hot charcoal and leave to cool. Strain the syrup through a sieve lined with a piece of muslin cloth.

Whilst the coals are still hot, lightly char a strip of orange zest, give it a twist and leave to cool.

Fill a rocks glass with a couple of large ice cubes and set aside to chill. Pour the bourbon, single malt, charcoal syrup and bitters into a mixing glass or jug filled with ice. Stir for 30 seconds, then strain into the chilled rocks glass and garnish with the cherry and burnt orange twist.

TROIS POMMES

'Haute comme trois pommes' ('as tall as three apples') describes someone of short stature and is such a fitting name for this drink, which has a lovely apple flavour and is very short.

MAKES 1 | PREP TIME: 5 MINUTES

50ml calvados
25ml rye whisky
25ml triple sec
25ml fresh lemon juice
4 drops citrus bitters
ice

TO GARNISH
1 maraschino cherry
lemon twist

Pour all the cocktail ingredients into a shaker filled with ice and shake vigorously.

Strain into a chilled coupe and garnish with the cherry and the lemon twist.

SMOKED ESPRESSO MARTINI

A little bit of planning is needed here; make your espresso and chill it well in advance. If you use hot coffee, you'll melt too much ice and end up with a weak, watery drink.

MAKES 1 | PREP TIME: 5 MINUTES

ice
45ml Smoked Vodka
    (see below)
45ml brewed dark roast
    espresso, chilled
30ml Kahlúa
2 coffee beans, to garnish

Fill a cocktail shaker with ice, add the Smoked Vodka, espresso and Kahlúa and shake vigorously for a minute.

Drain the martini glass. Strain into a chilled martini glass and garnish with the coffee beans.

SMOKED VODKA

I'm a big fan of subtle smoky cocktails, so I wanted to try smoking alcohol. As it's pretty neutral, vodka seemed the obvious place to start. The main issue with smoking vodka is evaporation; you need to expose as great a surface area as possible to the smoke, while minimising the loss of alcohol vapours. As well as being very accepting of flavours, vodka can be relatively inexpensive, so if you experiment and fail, it won't break the bank. I've found oak and maple work the best, the former gives a stronger, deeper smoky flavour; the latter more subtle and sweet. Use the vodka in a Smoked Espresso Martini (see above), or try it chilled over ice or mixed into a simple martini.

MAKES 500ML | PREP TIME: 5 MINUTES | COOK TIME: 6 HOURS

500ml vodka
ice cubes

You will need a pack of
    oak or maple smoking
    wood dust (see page 12).

Prepare the barbecue or smoker for cold smoking (see page 12). Pour the vodka into a small foil tray and then set that in a larger foil tray or baking tray half-filled with cold water and ice.

Set the trays on the grill, close the lid and smoke for 6 hours. During the smoking, gently stir the vodka every couple of hours to help the smoke permeate the liquid.

Decant the smoked vodka into a sterilised bottle (or reuse the original bottle), seal and chill.

APPLE and BASIL GINGER BEER

Proper ginger beer requires time, patience and a fairly intricate knowledge of brewing, none of which I possess. I discovered this the hard way after a fairly loud explosion and a kitchen covered in sticky ginger fizz. However I was determined to make it work. Try to find a proper sparkling apple juice rather than fizzy apple drink, otherwise it will be far too sweet.

MAKES 1.4 LITRES | PREP TIME: 10 MINUTES PLUS INFUSING | COOK TIME: 5 MINUTES

150g granulated sugar
125ml water
75g fresh ginger, unpeeled and coarsely grated
juice of 1–2 lemons, to taste
1 litre sparkling apple juice

TO SERVE
crushed ice
1 large bunch of basil, leaves picked

Put the sugar, water and ginger into a saucepan and bring to the boil, then reduce and heat and simmer for 3 minutes until the sugar has completely dissolved, stirring occasionally. Set aside to cool and then leave to infuse for an hour.

Squeeze half the lemon juice into the ginger syrup and then strain through a fine sieve lined with a piece of muslin cloth into a jug, squeezing out as much liquid as possible. Cover with clingfilm and chill until you're ready to serve.

Combine the syrup and sparkling apple juice in a large jug and taste; if it's a little on the sweet side, add more lemon juice.

To serve, fill tall glasses with crushed ice and a few basil leaves – give them a slap between the palms of your hands to really release the flavour – then pour the apple ginger beer over the top.

LEMONADE

Proper lemonade knocks spots off anything you can buy. It's deliciously refreshing simply served over ice with a sprig of mint, or try adding a splash of gin and a sprig of rosemary.

MAKES 1.4 LITRES | PREP TIME: 10 MINUTES | COOK TIME: 5 MINUTES

8 large unwaxed lemons
150g caster sugar
pinch of fine sea salt
150ml water

TO SERVE
ice
sprigs of mint
1 litre sparkling water, or to taste

Using a sharp potato peeler, peel the zest from 3 of the lemons; if you pick up any of the pith, score it away with the back of a knife. Put the zest into a saucepan with the sugar, salt and water and bring to the boil, then reduce the heat and simmer for 3 minutes, stirring occasionally, until the sugar has completely dissolved. Remove from the heat and leave to infuse for an hour.

Squeeze the juice from all the lemons straight into the syrup (don't worry about catching the pips). Stir then strain through a fine-meshed sieve into a jug. At this point you can pour the liquid into a sterilised bottle, seal and transfer it to the fridge until required.

When you're ready to serve, pour the syrup over ice in a tall glass, add a sprig of mint and top up with sparkling water to taste. Or pour the syrup into a large jug, add sparkling water to top up to 2 litres, throw in a couple of handfuls of ice and some sprigs of mint and let everyone help themselves.

DESSERTS

TOASTED MARSHMALLOW
ICE CREAM

Although it's hard to beat a good toasted marshmallow, I've always wanted to take that delicious flavour of the crisp, smoky exterior and sweet, fluffy middle and use it in a dessert. Ice cream seemed like the obvious choice.

MAKES 1 LITRE | PREP TIME: 10 MINUTES PLUS CHILLING AND FREEZING | COOK TIME: 25 MINUTES

250g white marshmallows, halved if using large ones
ice
300ml double cream
6 large egg yolks
450ml whole milk (creamy Jersey milk works best)
1 tablespoon vanilla extract
pinch of fine sea salt

You will need metal or wooden skewers; if you're using wooden skewers, soak them in warm water for at least an hour.

Preheat the barbecue for direct grilling (see page 11). Thread the marshmallows onto skewers and toast them over the coals until they turn a deep brown all over; the trick is to keep them fairly high above the coals and keep rotating them so that they caramelise slowly. Try not to set them on fire, as this will make the ice cream bitter, although a few charred edges are more than acceptable. Set aside to cool.

Half-fill a large bowl with ice and water, set a slightly smaller bowl on top and pour in the cream. Tip the egg yolks into a separate bowl. Heat the milk, vanilla and salt in a saucepan until just simmering, then remove from the heat and pour onto the egg yolks, whisking constantly. Rinse out the pan, then pour in the milk mixture and set over a gentle heat. Cook very gently, stirring constantly with a heatproof rubber spatula, until the mixture has thickened enough to coat the back of a spoon. If you have a digital thermometer, the mixture should reach about 75°C.

As soon as the custard is ready, remove the pan from the heat and pour it into the jug of a liquidiser; it's really important not to hang around, as even the residual heat of the pan will overcook the yolks and split the custard. Add the toasted marshmallows to the hot custard, cover with the lid and leave to stand for 10 minutes; this will melt the marshmallows and give you a lovely smooth ice cream. Blend the custard and marshmallows until smooth, then pour onto the chilled cream and stir to combine. Cover with clingfilm and chill in the fridge overnight.

The next day, churn the mixture in an ice-cream maker until frozen, then scoop into cones and serve. If you want to be really flash, you can quickly scorch the top of the ice cream with a blowtorch as you serve it.

SALTED CARAMEL ICE CREAM

The combination of creamy milk, sweet caramel and sea salt in this ice cream is a nod to long summers spent in Brittany, famed for its delicious caramels au beurre salé. Measure the salt accurately, as too much will prevent the ice cream from freezing properly.

MAKES 1 LITRE │ PREP TIME: 5 MINUTES PLUS CHILLING AND FREEZING │ COOK TIME: 30 MINUTES

ice
6 large egg yolks
450ml whole milk (creamy
   Jersey milk works best)
1 tablespoon vanilla extract
1 level teaspoon sea salt flakes
200g caster sugar
300ml double cream

FOR THE CARAMEL PIECES
sunflower oil, for greasing
150g caster sugar
75ml water
1 teaspoon sea salt flakes

Half-fill a large bowl with ice and water, and set a slightly smaller bowl on top. Tip the egg yolks into a separate bowl. Heat the milk, vanilla and salt in a saucepan until just simmering, then remove from the heat and pour onto the egg yolks, whisking constantly. Rinse out the pan, then pour in the milk mixture and set over a gentle heat. Cook very gently, stirring constantly with a heatproof rubber spatula, until the mixture has thickened enough to coat the back of a spoon. If you have a digital thermometer, the mixture should reach about 75°C. Keep an eye on it, as the mixture can easily scramble. As soon as the custard is ready, remove the pan from the heat and pour it into the chilled bowl.

Tip the caster sugar into a large, non-stick frying pan and set over a medium heat. Cook gently for 3–4 minutes, tilting and swirling the pan, until the sugar has melted. Cook for a further couple of minutes until the caramel has turned a deep amber colour, then remove from the heat and carefully pour the cream over. Be careful, as the mixture can spatter. When the cream hits the caramel, it will all go into shock and the caramel will set hard, but don't fret – this is supposed to happen. Return the pan to the heat and cook gently for a couple of minutes, stirring with the heatproof rubber spatula, until the caramel has melted and you have a smooth, golden brown liquid. Pour this on top of the custard mixture and stir to combine. Transfer the mixture to a large jug, cover with clingfilm and refrigerate overnight.

The next day, make the caramel. Line a baking tray with a heatproof silicone mat or a lightly oiled sheet of baking parchment. Bring the sugar and water to the boil in a large, non-stick frying pan and boil for 7–8 minutes. As soon it reaches that same dark amber colour as for the ice cream, pour it out onto the lined tray. Immediately sprinkle over the salt, then tilt the tray to help spread the caramel as thinly as possible. Leave to cool completely, then use a rolling pin to break into small pieces.

Remove the ice-cream mixture from the fridge and give it a quick whisk, then churn in an ice-cream maker until frozen. Beat in the caramel pieces, spoon into a plastic container and freeze until you're ready to serve. The ice cream is ready to eat straight away, but the caramel pieces will start to soften and turn deliciously gooey after a day or two.

TOFFEE APPLE ICE CREAM

Ice cream is a great vehicle for flavour and I like taking familiar desserts or sweets and replicating them in ice-cream form. This is a grown-up take on a childhood treat that I've always associated with bonfire night, so it makes sense to serve it after a barbecue while you sit and chat next to the slowly dying embers. If you're off the booze, or want to make it child-friendly, you can leave out the Calvados.

MAKES 1 LITRE | PREP TIME: 10 MINUTES PLUS CHILLING AND FREEZING | COOK TIME: 20 MINUTES

ice
300ml double cream
6 large egg yolks
100g caster sugar
450ml whole milk (creamy
    Jersey milk works best)
2 teaspoons vanilla extract
pinch of fine sea salt
50ml Calvados or apple brandy

**FOR THE CARAMELISED
    APPLES**
100g caster sugar
2 Granny Smith apples, peeled,
    cored and finely chopped
25g lightly salted butter
juice of ½ lemon

Half-fill a large bowl with ice and water, set a slightly smaller bowl on top and pour in the cream. Whisk together the egg yolks and sugar in a separate bowl. Heat the milk, vanilla and salt in a saucepan until just simmering, then remove from the heat and pour onto the egg yolks, whisking constantly. Rinse out the pan, then pour in the milk mixture and set over a gentle heat. Cook very gently, stirring constantly with a heatproof rubber spatula, until the mixture has thickened enough to coat the back of a spoon. If you have a digital thermometer, the mixture should reach about 75°C.

As soon as the custard is ready, remove the pan from the heat and pour it into the chilled cream. Stir for 3–4 minutes to cool the mixture, then pour into a large jug. Stir in the Calvados, cover with clingfilm and refrigerate overnight.

Meanwhile, make the caramelised apples. Put the sugar into a large, non-stick frying pan and heat gently until it turns a deep caramel colour. Add the chopped apples and cook for 3–4 minutes until they start to turn translucent. Stir in the butter and lemon juice and cook for a further minute, then remove from the heat and leave to cool completely. Transfer to a small bowl, cover with clingfilm and chill in the fridge.

Remove the ice-cream mixture from the fridge and give it a quick whisk, then churn in an ice-cream maker until frozen. Stir in the caramelised apples and then spoon into a plastic container and freeze until you're ready to serve.

COLONEL

A sharp lemon sorbet is a great way to round off a barbecue, but combined with a glug of ice-cold vodka it might just get the party started all over again. Rather than an excuse to get sloshed after dinner, this is actually a traditional dessert digestif on menus all over France. Good lemons (the unwaxed, Sicilian ones) and a decent, ice-cold vodka are crucial.

MAKES 1 LITRE | PREP TIME: 10 MINUTES PLUS COOLING AND FREEZING | COOK TIME: 5 MINUTES

500ml water
150g caster sugar
50g glucose syrup
6–8 unwaxed lemons
2 tablespoons ice-cold
   vodka, plus extra to serve

Pour the water, sugar and glucose syrup into a saucepan. Using a sharp potato peeler, peel the zest from 3 of the lemons and add to the plan; if you pick up any of the pith, score it away with the back of a knife, otherwise the sorbet will taste bitter. Bring the liquid to the boil, and as soon as the sugar has dissolved, remove the pan from the heat and leave to cool completely.

Meanwhile, squeeze the remaining lemons through a sieve into a large measuring jug; you need 300ml juice. Once the syrup has cooled, pour through a sieve onto the measured lemon juice and stir to combine. Stir in the vodka, then churn in an ice-cream maker until frozen.

To serve, put a scoop of sorbet into a chilled serving glass or bowl and pour over a good slug of ice-cold vodka.

LEMON SHERBET PAVLOVA

My mum is a brilliant cook and makes a great pavlova. It's always beautifully crisp on the outside with a pillowy soft, slightly chewy centre. I wanted to combine this with another childhood favourite, lemon sherbet. The sherbet is very simple to make and has created a real buzz every time I've served it. Make sure you wait until the very last minute to sprinkle it over the pavlova so that you don't lose any of the fizz.

SERVES 6 | PREP TIME: 25 MINUTES PLUS COOLING | COOK TIME: 2 HOURS

FOR THE SHERBET
3 unwaxed lemons
2 teaspoons vitamin C powder
2 teaspoons caster sugar

FOR THE MERINGUE
50g icing sugar
150g caster sugar
4 large egg whites
pinch of fine sea salt

FOR THE TOPPING
450ml double cream,
   whipped to soft peaks
150g sharp lemon curd

Preheat the oven to 120°C/gas mark ½. Using a fine grater, grate the zest of the lemons in an even layer onto a flat baking tray lined with greaseproof paper. Set aside while you make the meringue.

Sift the icing sugar into a bowl and combine with the caster sugar. Whisk the egg whites and sea salt in a stand mixer fitted with a whisk attachment or with an electric hand whisk to form soft peaks. Gradually whisk in the sugars, then whisk on a high speed for a further 2 minutes until stiff and glossy.

Line a large, flat baking tray with greaseproof paper; if the paper is being particularly unruly, use a little meringue mixture to stick down the corners. Spoon the meringue mixture onto the paper and use the back of a spoon to spread out into a large circle. Put the meringue and lemon zest trays into the oven and bake them for an hour. Remove the lemon zest from the oven and set aside to cool, leaving the meringue in the oven for a further hour. Turn off the oven and leave the meringue for a further 30 minutes. Then open the oven door and leave the meringue to cool completely. This will result in a really crisp meringue with no cracking or weeping.

While the meringue is cooling, make the sherbet. Grind the dried lemon zest, vitamin C powder and sugar to a fine powder using a pestle and mortar or a spice grinder.

Spoon the whipped cream over the top of the meringue, then drop spoonfuls of lemon curd over the top. Using the tip of a butter knife, swirl the cream and lemon curd together to create a rippled effect. Just before serving, sprinkle over the sherbet.

HONEY ROAST FIGS with
BLACK PEPPER MASCARPONE

I love figs in every form, be it torn through a crisp salad with some salty cured ham or gently roasted to jammy perfection. The warming spice of the black pepper does a great job here, pairing really well with the sweetness of the honey and figs. And if you've never used olive oil in a dessert before, this is a great chance to see how well it works; use a fruity, peppery one to match the flavours of the rest of the dish.

SERVES 4 | PREP TIME: 10 MINUTES | COOK TIME: 10 MINUTES

6 large ripe figs
20g lightly salted butter
2 tablespoons orange blossom
   honey or other floral honey

FOR THE MASCARPONE
150g mascarpone
1 tablespoon icing sugar, sifted
½ teaspoon freshly ground
   black pepper

TO SERVE
2 tablespoons toasted pine nuts
extra virgin olive oil

Preheat the barbecue for direct grilling (see page 11). Trim the stalks from the figs and cut each in half lengthways. Lay out a large sheet of foil, butter one half and lay the figs cut-side up on top. Drizzle the honey over the figs, then fold the empty half of the foil over the top and seal the edges to make a neat parcel. Lay on the grill, close the lid and cook for 10 minutes.

Meanwhile, beat together the mascarpone, icing sugar and pepper in a bowl until smooth.

Serve the figs with the black pepper mascarpone, topped with the pine nuts and a drizzle of extra virgin olive oil.

GRILLED PINEAPPLE
with TOASTED BRIOCHE

Pineapple grills so beautifully; it holds together well and a light charring enhances its natural tropical sweetness. The spiced rum caramel doubles as a glaze and then a sauce at the end, but it can burn easily while you're grilling, so keep the pineapple moving as it cooks.

SERVES 4 | PREP TIME: 10 MINUTES | COOK TIME: 20 MINUTES

150g caster sugar
75ml water
3 star anise
4 tablespoons dark rum
1 large pineapple, peeled,
    cored and quartered

FOR THE VANILLA CREAM
300ml double cream
1 tablespoon icing sugar, sifted
1 vanilla pod, split lengthways
    and seeds scraped out
1 tablespoon dark rum

TO SERVE
4 slices of brioche
25g unsalted butter, melted

You will need 4 metal or wooden skewers; if you're using wooden skewers, soak them in warm water for at least an hour.

Combine the vanilla cream ingredients in a large bowl and whip to soft peaks. Cover with clingfilm and chill until needed.

Bring the sugar, water and star anise to the boil in a large, non-stick frying pan and boil for 7–8 minutes until it just reaches a dark amber colour. Immediately remove from the heat and stir in the rum.

Preheat the barbecue for direct grilling (see page 11). Thread each pineapple quarter onto a skewer, brush with the caramel and grill for 7–8 minutes until softened and lightly charred, turning regularly and brushing with the caramel. Remove from the heat and give a final brush with the caramel.

Brush the brioche slices with melted butter and lightly toast on the barbecue. Serve the pineapple with the toasted brioche, vanilla cream and a drizzle of any leftover caramel.

ROAST CHERRIES with VANILLA

These boozy roast cherries perfumed with vanilla make a delicious dessert when spooned over a good vanilla ice cream. Regular brandy, dark rum or bourbon all work well as substitutes for the cherry brandy.

SERVES 4 | **PREP TIME: 10 MINUTES PLUS MARINATING** | **COOK TIME: 15 MINUTES**

3 tablespoons cherry brandy
2 tablespoons dark muscovado
   sugar
1 vanilla pod, spilt lengthways
   and seeds scraped out
500g cherries, stoned

TO SERVE
vanilla ice cream
2 shortbread or other buttery
   biscuits, crumbled

Combine the brandy, sugar and vanilla seeds in a large bowl and whisk together until the sugar has dissolved. Add the cherries and toss to combine, then set aside to marinate at room temperature for at least 2 hours.

If you're making this at the end of the meal on a charcoal barbecue, remove the grill and even out the embers. Otherwise preheat the barbecue and remove the grill. If you're using a gas barbecue, reduce the heat to low. Take a large sheet of foil, about 50cm long, and fold it in half away from you. Fold in the sides to make a pouch, then open it out at the mouth; you should have a foil bag, open at the top. Pour the cherries and all the liquid into the bag, then fold the opening over to seal tightly. The parcel should be big enough, when laid flat, for the cherries to sit in one even layer. Lay the parcel on the embers or on the grill and cook for 15 minutes, turning and rotating occasionally. Take care to avoid piercing the bag, otherwise you'll lose all the lovely syrup.

Remove the bag from the heat and leave to cool for a couple of minutes, then carefully open and pour the contents into a bowl. Spoon the hot cherries and syrup over vanilla ice cream and top with the biscuit crumbs.

SALTED CHOCOLATE PRALINE S'MORES

When we finish cooking on the barbecue there is often still plenty of life left in the coals, so I always have a stash of huge American marshmallows for everyone to toast over the glowing embers. And you can guarantee that at least one person will set theirs on fire. I wanted a fun recipe that gets everyone involved at the end of a meal, and so this jazzed-up version of the campfire classic was born.

SERVES 16 | **PREP TIME: 20 MINUTES PLUS COOLING AND CHILLING** | **COOK TIME: 15 MINUTES**

FOR THE PRALINE
75g caster sugar
75g flaked almonds
150g dark chocolate
    (70 per cent cocoa solids),
    broken into pieces
pinch of sea salt flakes

TO ASSEMBLE
16 large marshmallows
32 digestive biscuits

You will need metal or wooden skewers; if you're using wooden skewers, soak them in warm water for at least an hour.

For the praline, heat the sugar in a large, non-stick frying pan until melted, swirling and tilting the pan occasionally to ensure that it melts evenly. As soon as the caramel has turned a deep brown colour, stir in the flaked almonds and cook for a further 2 minutes. Pour onto a baking tray lined with a heatproof silicone mat or a lightly oiled sheet of baking parchment. Leave to cool completely, then break into chunks.

Meanwhile, melt the chocolate in a heatproof bowl set over a pan of gently simmering water.

Put the caramel chunks into a food processor and blend for 5 minutes. Your food processor will probably rattle around all over the place for the first couple of minutes, so hold it down to stop it bouncing away, but once the praline gets finer, you should be able to leave it alone. Keep blending until the mixture turns to a paste; when it looks like runny peanut butter, it's ready.

Beat the praline into the melted chocolate, then stir in the salt and leave to cool and thicken. Spoon it onto a sheet of clingfilm and roll into a log about 4cm in diameter, then chill in the fridge for about an hour until firm. Slice into 16 rounds and chill until you're ready to serve.

Thread the marshmallows onto skewers and toast them over the coals until golden and crisp on the outside. Sandwich each one along with a praline round between two digestive biscuits.

RESTOKE
THE FIRE

BRUNCH PIZZETTE

The first time I made these, I cursed myself for not having done so sooner. It's such an obvious way to serve all the elements of a great brunch – eggs, bacon, tomatoes, avocado and chilli – but hand-held and ready in a flash. Make sure your barbecue is really hot so that the bases cook quickly enough to leave your egg yolks beautifully runny.

MAKES 8 | PREP TIME: 30 MINUTES PLUS RISING | COOK TIME: ABOUT 5 MINUTES

FOR THE DOUGH
400g strong white bread flour
100g fine semolina, plus extra
    for dusting
7g sachet fast-action dried yeast
1½ teaspoons fine sea salt
1 tablespoon honey
330ml lager
olive oil, for greasing

FOR THE SAUCE
2 tablespoons extra virgin
    olive oil
2 garlic cloves, crushed
pinch of chilli flakes
600g good-quality Italian
    canned chopped tomatoes
pinch of caster sugar
pinch of fine sea salt

FOR THE PANCETTA AND
ROSEMARY PIZZETTE
125g buffalo mozzarella,
    torn into small pieces
12 wafer-thin slices of
    smoked pancetta
2 sprigs of rosemary,
    leaves chopped
4 medium eggs

FOR THE AVOCADO
AND CHILLI PIZZETTE
125g buffalo mozzarella,
    torn into small pieces
2 red chillies, finely chopped
4 medium eggs
1 ripe avocado, stoned,
    peeled and diced
juice of 1 lime

fine sea salt
a small handful of
    coriander leaves

For the dough, combine the dry ingredients and honey in the bowl of a stand mixer fitted with a dough hook. Start the machine on a low speed and pour in the lager. Knead on a low speed for 3 minutes, then increase the speed to the next setting and knead for a further 6 minutes. If you're making the dough by hand, combine the ingredients in a large mixing bowl to form a rough dough. Tip out onto a clean work surface and knead for 10 minutes.

Transfer the dough to a large bowl, lightly greased with olive oil, and cover with a clean tea towel. Leave in a warm place for an hour or until the dough has doubled in size. Fire up the barbecue to a high temperature ready for direct grilling (see page 11).

While the dough is busying itself, make the sauce. Heat the oil in a saucepan over a very low heat, add the garlic and chilli flakes and cook gently for 2 minutes. Add the tomatoes, sugar and salt and bring to a gentle simmer. Cook for 10 minutes, then remove from the heat and leave to cool.

Set a pizza stone or heavy baking tray on the grill, close the lid and open the vents as wide as possible. Dust the work surface with semolina, turn the dough out and divide into eight equal balls. Cover with a clean, damp tea towel to prevent the dough from drying out. Roll each ball out thinly to make a small round, then spread with the cooled tomato sauce.

For the pancetta and rosemary pizzette, divide the mozzarella, pancetta and rosemary between four dough rounds, leaving space for an egg in the centre of each. Use a pizza peel or thin, flat baking tray to lift the pizzette from the work surface and slide them onto the hot pizza stone or heavy baking tray. Crack an egg onto each pizzette, then close the lid and bake for 3–4 minutes (depending on how hot you can make your barbecue) until the pancetta is crispy.

For the avocado and chilli pizzette, divide the mozzarella and chillies between the remaining dough rounds, leaving space for an egg in the centre of each. Transfer onto the hot pizza stone or heavy baking tray as above and crack an egg onto each pizzette, then close the lid and bake for 3–4 minutes until the cheese is golden and bubbling. Slide the pizzette onto a board, top with the diced avocado and squeeze a little lime juice over each. Finish each pizzette with a pinch of salt and a few coriander leaves.

BAKED EGGS with MERGUEZ

This vibrant breakfast dish has all the components of a great cooked breakfast – sausages, tomatoes and eggs – but with plenty of fragrant spices and chilli to really wake you up and kick any hangover into touch. Merguez sausages are the star of the show here; either beef or lamb (or sometimes a combination of both) and flavoured with fiery harissa, garlic and a whole host of spices. I make this in a big old cast-iron pan, stick it in the middle of the table with some crusty bread and let everyone dive in.

SERVES 4 │ PREP TIME: 10 MINUTES PLUS COOLING │ COOK TIME: ABOUT 30 MINUTES

800g ripe tomatoes
olive oil, for frying
1 onion, finely chopped
pinch of chilli flakes
1 garlic clove, crushed
1 teaspoon ras el hanout
2 teaspoons tomato purée
8 merguez sausages
4 medium eggs
hot smoked paprika,
    for sprinkling
crusty bread, to serve

Preheat the barbecue for direct grilling (see page 11). Lay the tomatoes on the grill and cook for 10 minutes until charred and softened, turning regularly. Set aside to cool, then roughly chop.

Set a heavy-based frying pan on the grill, add a splash of oil and fry the onion and chilli flakes for 5 minutes until the onion starts to soften. Add the garlic and cook for a couple of minutes, then add the ras el hanout and fry for a minute. Stir in the tomato purée, add the chopped tomatoes and mix together, then move the pan to a cooler part of the grill and leave to bubble away gently.

Lay the sausages on the grill and cook for 6–8 minutes until cooked through, turning regularly.

Once the tomato sauce has thickened, make four wells in it with the back of a spoon and crack an egg into each. Close the lid and cook for 5–6 minutes until the whites are just set but the yolks are still runny. Sprinkle over a little hot smoked paprika and then serve with the merguez and crusty bread.

HUEVOS RANCHEROS
with CHORIZO

I love anything spicy for breakfast or brunch; it wakes up your palate, sets you up for the day and can help to right all sorts of wrongs from the night before. This spicy Mexican dish is based around three key elements: crisp tortillas, a spicy tomato sauce and eggs. I think most dishes can be improved by the addition of chorizo, so I always add some to my sauce.

SERVES 6 │ PREP TIME: 15 MINUTES PLUS COOLING │ COOK TIME: 35 MINUTES

FOR THE SAUCE
1 red pepper
5 ripe tomatoes
1 dried ancho chilli
1 dried chipotle chilli
olive oil, for frying
1 onion, finely chopped
1 garlic clove, crushed
pinch of caster sugar

TO SERVE
125g dry-cured chorizo,
    split lengthways
6 medium eggs
6 corn tortillas
1 small bunch of coriander,
    roughly chopped

Preheat the barbecue for direct grilling (see page 11). Lay the red pepper and tomatoes on the grill and cook for 10 minutes until charred and softened, turning regularly. Set aside to cool, then peel the pepper and roughly chop, along with the tomatoes.

Meanwhile, soak the dried chillies in boiling water for 10 minutes, then drain, deseed and finely chop.

Set a heavy-based frying pan on the grill, add a splash of oil and fry the onion and garlic for 5 minutes until they start to soften. Add the chopped peppers and tomatoes and stir together, then move the pan to a cooler part of the grill and leave to bubble away gently for 10 minutes. Pour the sauce into a liquidiser, add the sugar and blend until smooth. Return to the pan and set on the edge of the grill to keep warm.

Lay the chorizo on the grill and cook for 5 minutes until crisp, turning regularly. Chop finely and add to the sauce.

Fry the eggs in a little olive oil in a frying pan. Meanwhile, heat the corn tortillas on the grill for a minute on each side until crisp.

To serve, spoon a little sauce onto each tortilla, top with a fried egg and spoon on more of the sauce. Finish each serving with a little chopped coriander.

LOBSTER BENEDICT

Every now and again it's good to go large and splash out on some top-quality ingredients, crack open the Champagne and start the weekend in style. My theory is that you'd easily spend more money on going out for brunch than you would on the ingredients in this recipe and a bottle of fizz, and nobody frowns if you eat lobster in your pants at home.

SERVES 4 | PREP TIME: 10 MINUTES PLUS FREEZING | COOK TIME: 30 MINUTES

2 lobster, weighing 500g each
8 medium eggs, as fresh
    as possible
ice
25g lightly salted butter, melted

FOR THE HOLLANDAISE
2 egg yolks
2 tablespoons water
125g lightly salted butter,
    diced, plus extra to serve
squeeze of lemon juice
sea salt

TO SERVE
4 English muffins
pinch of cayenne pepper
1 small bunch of chives,
    finely chopped

To kill the lobsters humanely, first put them in the freezer for 30 minutes to render them unconscious. Meanwhile, preheat the barbecue for direct grilling (see page 11). Remove the lobsters from the freezer and cover them with a couple of cold, wet tea towels, leaving the heads exposed. Push the tip of a large, sharp knife through the cross on the top of the head; do this in one swift, purposeful movement and you'll kill the lobster instantly.

Bring a large pan of unsalted water to a gentle simmer, crack in the eggs and poach for 3–4 minutes until the whites are just set. Carefully transfer to a bowl of iced water and set aside.

For the hollandaise, put the egg yolks and water into a heavy-based saucepan and cook gently for 3–4 minutes, whisking constantly. When the yolks start to thicken, add all the butter and cook for 5 minutes, again whisking constantly. Do this over a gentle heat; as the butter melts, the yolks will cool and everything will come together into a smooth, silky sauce. Once the butter has melted, cook for a further 2 minutes until thickened, then remove from the heat and whisk in a little lemon juice to loosen the sauce. Season to taste with salt, cover and set aside.

Cut the lobsters in half lengthways and brush the cut sides with some of the melted butter. Place the lobsters cut-side down on the grill and cook for 3–4 minutes, then turn, brush with more butter and cook for a further 3 minutes. Twist off the tails and remove from the grill, leaving the claws on for another 2–3 minutes. Carefully lift the meat from the tails, then crack the claws with a sharp knife or lobster cracker and pull out the meat.

Split the muffins and toast lightly on the barbecue, then butter and divide between four serving plates. Top each muffin half with lobster meat and a poached egg, then spoon over the hollandaise. Finish with the cayenne pepper and chopped chives.

HOT-SMOKED SALMON
with SCRAMBLED EGGS

Hot smoking is a great way to cook salmon and is ready in a fraction of the time of the cold-smoked variety. It still needs to be cured, but if you make a start the night before, it's really quick the next morning, making it the perfect, impressive brunch dish.

SERVES 6 | PREP TIME: 10 MINUTES PLUS CURING | COOK TIME: 25 MINUTES

500g centre-cut piece of
   salmon fillet, skin on,
   pin bones removed
2 teaspoons fine sea salt
1 teaspoon demerara sugar

FOR THE EGGS
50g unsalted butter
8 large eggs, beaten
sea salt and freshly ground
   black pepper

TO SERVE
bagels or sourdough toast
1 small bunch of chives,
   finely chopped

You will need a large handful
of wood chips (see page 12),
soaked in warm water for
30 minutes.

The night before you plan to cook, lay the salmon on a large piece of clingfilm. Combine the salt and sugar in a small bowl and apply all over the salmon in an even layer. Wrap the salmon tightly in the clingfilm and lay in a tray large enough to catch any liquid that may escape. Place in the fridge overnight.

The next morning, unwrap the salmon and rinse off the cure under cold running water. Pat as dry as possible with plenty of kitchen paper, then lay flesh-side up on a wire rack and return to the fridge, uncovered, while you set up the barbecue or smoker for indirect grilling (see page 11).

Lay the fish on the grill skin-side down, close the lid and smoke for 20 minutes or until just cooked through. Remove from the heat and set aside to rest for a few minutes.

Heat the butter in a heavy-based pan over a medium heat. Add the eggs and, using a heatproof spatula, keep moving them around the pan, scraping the base and sides constantly; the key to great scrambled eggs is cooking them really gently and keeping them moving so that they cook evenly. When the eggs look like they're nearly ready, remove the pan from the heat and continue to stir for a minute; the residual heat in the pan will continue cooking them. Season to taste.

Flake the salmon and serve with the scrambled eggs and bagels or sourdough toast, scattered with the chopped chives.

SMOKED PORK BEANS
on TOAST

Making your own smoky beans is surprisingly simple, and if you foresee a bit of a fuzzy head, you can get them ready the night before. I use the thick slabs of smoked pork belly available in Polish delis; it saves loads of time and crisps up beautifully on the barbecue.

SERVES 4 | PREP TIME: 5 MINUTES | COOK TIME: 20 MINUTES

400g smoked pork belly,
  cut into thick slices
sea salt
Hot Sauce (page 128) or
  Tabasco sauce, to taste

FOR THE BEANS
400g can chopped tomatoes
2 x 400g cans cannellini
  beans, drained
2 tablespoons honey
2 tablespoons sherry vinegar
2 tablespoons Worcestershire
  sauce
1 tablespoon dark brown
  soft sugar
1 tablespoon Dijon mustard
1 teaspoon sweet smoked
  paprika

TO SERVE
4 slices of sourdough bread
2 tablespoons melted butter

Preheat the barbecue for direct grilling (see page 11). Lay the pork belly on the grill and cook for 15 minutes until golden and crisp, turning occasionally.

While the pork is cooking, combine all the ingredients for the beans in a saucepan and set on the grill alongside the pork. Cook for 15 minutes until the sauce has thickened, stirring regularly.

Transfer the pork to a chopping board, cut into chunks and stir into the beans. Season with a little salt, then add the Hot Sauce or Tabasco to taste. Remove the pan from the heat and keep warm.

Brush the sourdough bread slices on both sides with the melted butter, lay on the grill and cook for a minute or two on each side until lightly charred.

Divide the toast between four serving plates, top with the beans and serve.

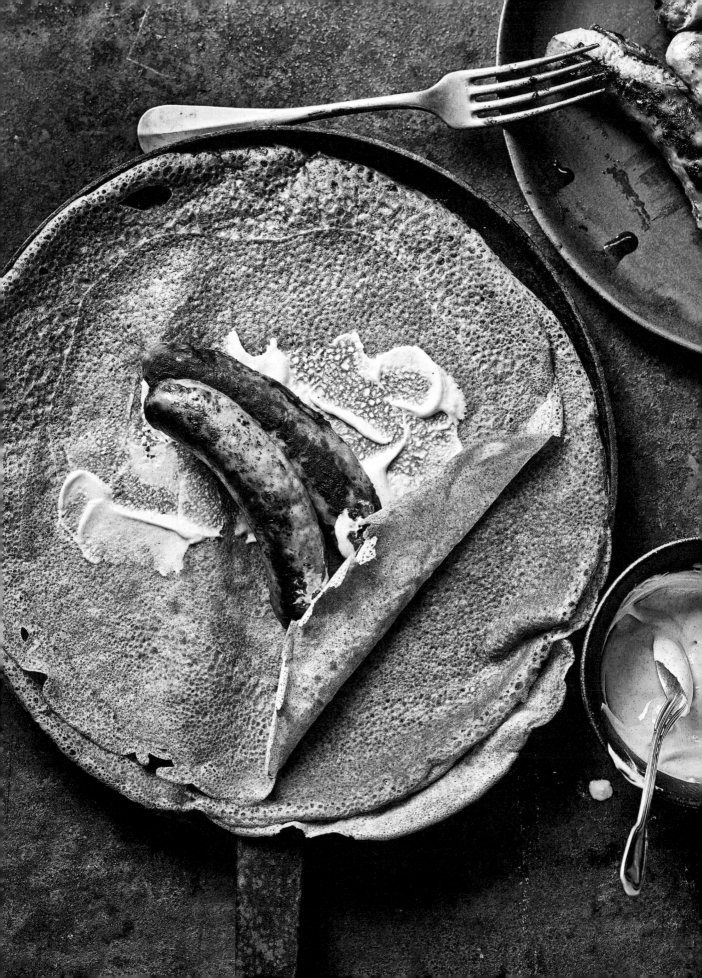

GALETTES SAUCISSES

This is a nod to family holidays spent in Brittany, where these buckwheat pancakes wrapped around sizzling-hot grilled sausages are something of an institution. Every time we'd go to the market, we'd head straight for the galette stall, watching with eager anticipation as the batter was deftly spread out with a wooden paddle to create huge crisp, lacy discs. There was always a charcoal barbecue with local garlicky sausages being turned, ready to be given a lick of mustard and wrapped in the savoury pancakes and handed over with a square of waxed paper to stop you burning your fingers. Simple and utterly delicious. The key is the buckwheat flour, which is essential for getting the right flavour and texture; it's just not a proper galette without it.

MAKES 8 | PREP TIME: 10 MINUTES PLUS RESTING | COOK TIME: 30 MINUTES

250g buckwheat flour (farine de blé noir de Bretagne)
½ teaspoon fine sea salt
250ml water
250ml whole milk, plus extra if needed (optional)
1 medium egg
50g salted butter, plus extra for frying
8 large Toulouse sausages or good-quality pork sausages
Dijon mustard, for spreading

Combine the flour and salt in a large mixing bowl and make a well in the centre. Whisk together the water, milk and egg in a jug, then pour into the well. Gradually incorporate the dry ingredients into the wet ingredients and whisk to a smooth batter. Cover with clingfilm and chill for at least an hour.

Meanwhile, to make a beurre noisette, melt the butter in a small saucepan over a medium heat. Continue to cook the butter until it turns a nut brown colour, then pour into a small jug.

Preheat the barbecue for direct grilling (see page 11). Remove the batter from the fridge, whisk in the cooled beurre noisette, then check the consistency – it should be the same as whipping cream. The longer it stands in the fridge, the thicker it will become, so just loosen it with a splash of milk or water.

Melt a little butter in a large, non-stick frying pan over a high heat, either on the hob or on the barbecue grill. Add a ladleful of the batter and quickly tilt and turn the pan so that it spreads evenly. Fry for 2 minutes on each side until lacy and golden brown. Transfer to a plate and continue with the remaining batter. Stack the galettes straight on top of each other as they're cooked; the residual steam will keep them soft and pliable.

Lay the sausages on the grill and cook for 10–15 minutes until cooked through, turning occasionally, then move to one side.

To assemble, quickly reheat a galette on the barbecue and spread one side with mustard. Lay a sausage on top, fold the bottom third of the galette up over the sausage and roll up. Half-wrap in a piece of greaseproof paper or foil (to make it easier to hold) and tuck in.

BUTTERMILK PANCAKES

A barbecue is a great way to feed pancakes to a crowd for brunch; I use an old, flat baking tray so that I can cook several at once while the bacon sizzles away around the outside of the grill. These pancakes are the thick, fluffy American variety and rely on the lift coming from the combination of baking powder and buttermilk. This means that the batter can't be made in advance, so make sure everything else is ready before you whisk it together.

SERVES 4 | PREP TIME: 10 MINUTES | COOK TIME: 20 MINUTES

12 rashers of thick-cut
  streaky bacon

FOR THE PANCAKES
300g plain flour
75g caster sugar
2 teaspoons baking powder
½ teaspoon fine sea salt
6 large eggs
250ml buttermilk
50g unsalted butter, melted
2 teaspoons vanilla extract
vegetable oil spray, for frying

maple syrup, to serve

Preheat the barbecue for direct grilling (see page 11). Grill the bacon for 3–4 minutes on each side until crisp, then wrap in foil and move to a cooler outer edge of the grill to keep warm.

Sift the flour, sugar, baking powder and salt into a large bowl and make a well in the centre. Whisk together the eggs, buttermilk, melted butter and vanilla extract in a large jug, then pour into the well. Gradually incorporate the dry ingredients into the wet ingredients and whisk to a smooth batter.

Lay a couple of sheets of foil on the grill, set your largest non-stick baking tray on top and spray it with oil. Fold a sheet of foil in half and set it to one side of the grill, ready to keep the cooked pancakes warm. Pour small ladlefuls of the batter onto the baking tray and fry gently for 1 minute or until bubbles start to appear on the surface. Flip and cook for a further minute, then transfer to the foil parcel to keep warm. Continue to cook the remaining batter in the same way.

Serve the pancakes with the crispy bacon and maple syrup.

MASALA CHAI

Before I visited India, I'd had what I thought was chai. However, after tasting a cup of boiling masala chai cooked over a huge wood fire in Jodhpur, I realised I'd never experienced the real thing. It's mesmerising watching the chai wallahs at work, adding spices, tea, milk and sugar to a constantly boiling vat of milk and water. I never take sugar in my tea, but the only way to drink masala chai is with plenty of sweetness.

SERVES 4 | PREP TIME: 5 MINUTES | COOK TIME 10 MINUTES

10 green cardamom pods, crushed
2 black cardamom pods, crushed
2 cinnamon stick, broken in half
6 thin slices of fresh ginger
8 cloves
1 teaspoon black peppercorns, crushed
300ml boiling water
300ml whole milk
1 tablespoon loose leaf black tea or 2 teabags torn open
sugar, to taste (I go for about 1 tablespoon)

Preheat the barbecue for direct grilling (see page 11). Set a heavy-based saucepan on the grill, add all the spices and toast for 2 minutes.

Pour over the boiling water and milk, stir in the tea and bring to a simmer. Cook for 5 minutes, stirring constantly, then remove from the heat and stir in sugar to taste.

Strain into glasses or cups and serve.

USEFUL LINKS

www.weber.com
For the best kettle barbecues and a great range of gas grills, smokers and accessories.

www.monolith-grill.de
For fantastic all-rounder ceramic kamado grills, with highly versatile cooking options and accurate temperature control; great for low and slow smoking, cold smoking, pizzas and traditional grilling.

www.macsbbq.com
One-stop shop for everything to do with barbecuing and smoking, including ProQ Cold Smoke Generators and smoking wood dust.

www.greenolivefirewood.co.uk
For natural hardwood chunks for smoking, lumpwood charcoal and eco firelighters.

www.theoxfordcharcoalcompany.co.uk
For sustainable British lumpwood charcoal from a wide range of woods.

www.coolchile.co.uk
Specialist Mexican food shop for top-notch dried chillies, tortillas and sauces.

www.japancentre.com
For specialist Japanese produce such as shichimi togarashi, seaweed, sake and condiments, and the Korean chilli paste gochujang.

www.souschef.co.uk
A treasure trove of specialist ingredients and equipment including kochukaru/gochugaru (Korean red chilli powder) for kimchi (see page 124).

INDEX

aioli, sesame 53
almonds: salted chocolate
    praline s'mores 183
anchovies
    salsa verde 129
    tuna niçoise as it should be 74
apple juice
    apple and basil ginger beer 167
    smoky bourbon barbecue
        sauce 129
apples
    fennel salad 78
    pickled apples 140
    toffee apple ice cream 174
aubergines
    aubergine and tomato sauce 38
    baba ganoush 120
avocados
    avocado and chilli pizzette 188
    guacamole 46

baba ganoush 120
bacon: cheese and bacon
    dogs 47
Bajan blackened fish kebabs 68
banana leaves, monkfish in 72
barbecue sauces
    quick sharp barbecue sauce 128
    smoky bourbon barbecue
        sauce 129
barbecues, types of 8
barrel smoker, offset 8
basil
    apple and basil ginger beer 167
    salsa verde 129
beans: smoked pork beans
    on toast 195
béarnaise sauce 131
beef 15
    beef short ribs with smoked
        beer 18
    brisket 134
    chilli cheese burgers 42
    chilli dogs 48
    chipotle steak tacos 46
    dry-rubbed sirloin of beef
        with burnt onions 20
    tomahawk steaks with blue
        cheese butter 22
beer, beef short ribs with
    smoked 18
beetroot juice: margarita
    de remolacha 160

biscuits: salted chocolate
    praline s'mores 183
bone marrow on toast,
    smoked 144
bourbon
    bourbon-glazed baby
        back ribs 50
    old smoky 164
    smoky bourbon sauce 129
bread
    flatbreads 117
    grilled panzanella 90
    pan con tomate 63
    potato rolls 115
    smoked bone marrow on
        toast 144
    smoked chicken salad 146
    smoked pork beans on toast 195
brioche, grilled pineapple with
    toasted 180
brisket 134
broccoli with gochujang
    and lemon 112
brunch pizzette 188
bulgar wheat: tabbouleh 106
bullet smoker 8
burgers
    chilli cheese burgers 42
    onion burger 56
butter
    blue cheese butter 22
    rosemary butter 25
    smoked butter 157
    smoked chilli butter 93
    thyme butter 150
buttermilk
    buttermilk dressing 146
    buttermilk onion rings 98
    buttermilk pancakes 199

cabbage
    chipotle slaw 101
    grilled red cabbage with hot
        and sour dressing 105
    kimchi 124
    pickled red cabbage 44
calvados: trois pommes 164
caramel: salted caramel ice
    cream 172
cardamom: masala chai 200
carrots
    chipotle slaw 101
    root vegetable slaw 18

sticky chilli pork belly with
    rice noodle salad 28
cauliflower: spiced cauliflower
    steaks with yogurt and tahini
    dressing 96
chai, masala 200
charcoal 12
cheese
    avocado and chilli pizzette 188
    baked cheese with Ratte
        potatoes 39
    blue cheese butter 22
    blue cheese dip 61
    cheese and bacon dogs 47
    chilli cheese burgers 42
    feta and chilli parcels with
        Greek salad 110
    grilled polenta with rosemary
        and Taleggio 38
    mac 'n' cheese 99
    'nduja pizza 54
    pancetta and rosemary
        pizzette 188
    roast radishes with crumbled
        Parmesan 102
    smoked Cheddar 157
    see also mascarpone
chermoula, spatchcock
    chicken with 33
cherries: roast cherries
    with vanilla 182
chicken 15
    chicken and salt 34
    chicken satay 60
    chicken wings with hot sauce
        and blue cheese 61
    green chicken kebabs 58
    jerk chicken 31
    smoked chicken 136
    smoked chicken salad 146
    spatchcock chicken with
        chermoula 33
chickpea, roast pepper and
    chorizo salad 109
chicory: chargrilled leaves with
    burnt lemon dressing 94
chillies
    avocado and chilli pizzette 188
    Bajan blackened fish kebabs 68
    blackened tomato salsa 122
    broccoli with gochujang
        and lemon 112
    chicken satay 60

chilli and garlic salt 83
chilli cheese burgers 42
chilli dogs 48
chimichurri 128
chipotle slaw 101
chipotle steak tacos with
    guacamole 46
feta and chilli parcels 110
grilled panzanella 90
hot sauce 128
huevos rancheros with
    chorizo 191
jerk chicken 31
monkfish in banana leaves 72
pickled green chillies 126
pico de gallo with charred
    corn 123
prawns and scallops with
    chilli and lime 70
rice noodle salad 28
smoked chilli butter 93
smoky bourbon barbecue
    sauce 129
sticky chilli pork belly 28
sweet chilli sauce 123
chimichurri 128
chimney starters 11, 15
Chinese leaf cabbage: kimchi 124
chipotle chillies
    chipotle slaw 101
    chipotle steak tacos 46
chocolate: salted chocolate
    praline s'mores 183
chorizo
    chickpea, roast pepper
        and chorizo salad 109
    chilli dogs 48
    huevos rancheros with
        chorizo 191
citrus salt 83
cocktails
    corn 'n' oil 162
    daiquiri 162
    margarita de remolacha 160
    margarita de toronja picante 160
    old smoky 164
    rum punch 162
    smoked espresso martini 166
    smoked vodka 166
    trois pommes 164
coffee: smoked espresso
    martini 166
cold smoking 12

colonel 175
coriander
    chermoula 33
    guacamole 46
    rice noodle salad 28
corn 'n' oil 162
corn on the cob: charred corn
    with smoked chilli butter 93
cream, vanilla 180
cucumber
    Greek salad 110
    mackerel with seaweed
        and mushroom salad 81
    tzatziki 122
cuttlefish: sepia a la plancha 84

daiquiri 162
dips
    baba ganoush 120
    blackened tomato salsa 122
    blue cheese dip 61
    pico de gallo with charred
        corn 123
    tzatziki 122
direct grilling 11
'dirty' cooking 25
    coal-roast sea bass with
        mussels 86
    dirty chops with rosemary
        butter and pickled fennel 25
    dirty Romesco sauce 149
disposable barbecues 8
dressings
    burnt lemon dressing 94
    buttermilk dressing 146
    hot and sour dressing 105
    yogurt and tahini dressing 96
drinks 160–167, 200

eggs
    avocado and chilli pizzette 188
    baked eggs with merguez 190
    béarnaise sauce 131
    buttermilk pancakes 199
    hot-smoked salmon with
        scrambled eggs 194
    huevos rancheros with
        chorizo 191
    lemon sherbet pavlova 176
    lobster benedict 192
    pancetta and rosemary
        pizzette 188
    salted caramel ice cream 172

toasted marshmallow ice
    cream 170
toffee apple ice cream 174
tuna niçoise as it should be 74
equipment 15

fennel
    fennel salad 78
    pickled fennel 25
    porchetta 30
    seafood paella 36
feta and chilli parcels with
    Greek salad 110
figs: honey roast figs with black
    pepper mascarpone 179
firelighters 12
fish
    Bajan blackened fish kebabs 68
    coal-roast sea bass with
        mussels 86
    hot-smoked salmon with
        scrambled eggs 194
    mackerel with seaweed and
        mushroom salad 81
    monkfish in banana leaves 72
    sea bass, Ibiza style 78
    smoked herrings 156
    smoked salmon 153
    tandoori sea bream with
        chopped kachumba 77
    teriyaki salmon 80
    tuna niçoise as it should be 74
flatbreads 117
foil trays 15
frankfurters
    cheese and bacon dogs 47
    chilli dogs 48
French beans: tuna niçoise
    as it should be 74
fuel 12

galangal: chicken satay 60
galettes saucisses 197
Galician octopus 66
garlic
    chickpea, roast pepper
        and chorizo salad 109
    chilli and garlic salt 83
    hot sauce 128
    hot-smoked garlic 152
    kimchi 124
    porchetta 30
    smoky bourbon sauce 129

gas barbecue 8
ginger beer, apple and basil 167
gloves, rubber 15
gouchujang: broccoli with
    gochujang and lemon 112
grapefruit
  citrus salt 83
  margarita de toronja picante 160
Greek salad 110
green chicken kebabs 58
grilling, direct vs indirect 11
grills, kamado 8, 11
guacamole 46

ham, coal-roast scallops with
    sweetcorn and Serrano 73
hay-smoked lamb with white
    onion purée 147
herrings, smoked 156
hollandaise sauce 192
honey roast figs with black
    pepper mascarpone 179
hot and sour dressing 105
hot sauce 61
hot smoking 11
huevos rancheros with
    chorizo 191

ice cream
  salted caramel ice cream 172
  toasted marshmallow ice
    cream 170
  toffee apple ice cream 174
indirect grilling 11

jerk chicken 31

kachumba, tandoori sea
    bream with chopped 77
kahlúa: smoked espresso
    martini 166
kamado grill 8, 11
kebabs
  Bajan blackened fish kebabs 68
  green chicken kebabs 58
  lamb shish kebabs 44
  pork souvlaki 57
ketchup, plum 26
kettle barbecue 8, 11
kidney beans: chilli dogs 48
kimchi 124

lamb 15

hay-smoked lamb with
    white onion purée 147
lamb shawarma 137
lamb shish kebabs with
    pickled red cabbage 44
spiced leg of lamb 23
sticky lamb ribs 51
lardo: smoked tomatoes with
    lardo di Colonnata 139
lemon curd: lemon sherbet
    pavlova 176
lemons
  broccoli with gochujang
    and lemon 112
  burnt lemon dressing 94
  chermoula 33
  citrus salt 83
  colonel 175
  lemon sherbet pavlova 176
  lemonade 167
lettuce
  chargrilled leaves with burnt
    lemon dressing 94
  lobster rolls 87
  smoked chicken salad 146
  tuna niçoise as it should be 74
limes
  daiquiri 162
  margarita de remolacha 160
  margarita de toronja
    picante 160
  prawns and scallops with
    chilli and lime 70
  rice noodle salad 28
  rum punch 162
lobster
  lobster benedict 192
  lobster rolls 87

mac 'n' cheese 99
mackerel with seaweed
    and mushroom salad 81
mango juice: rum punch 162
margaritas
  margarita de remolacha 160
  margarita de toronja picante 160
marshmallows
  salted chocolate praline
    s'mores 183
  toasted marshmallow ice
    cream 170
martini, smoked espresso 166
masala chai 200

mascarpone, honey roast figs
    with black pepper 179
matches 15
mayonnaise 131
merguez, baked eggs with 190
meringues: lemon sherbet
    pavlova 176
mint
  rice noodle salad 28
  salsa verde 129
  tabbouleh 106
  tzatziki 122
monkfish in banana leaves 72
mozzarella
  avocado and chilli pizzette 188
  'nduja pizza 54
  pancetta and rosemary pizzette 188
mushrooms: seaweed and
    mushroom salad 81
mussels
  coal-roast sea bass with
    mussels 86
  seafood paella 36

'nduja pizza 54
noodles: rice noodle salad 28

octopus, Galician 66
offset barrel smoker 8
old smoky 164
olives: Greek salad 110
onions
  burnt onions 20
  buttermilk onion rings 98
  hay-smoked lamb with
    white onion purée 147
  onion burger 56
  onion salad 137
  pink pickled onions 126
  smoked onions with thyme
    butter 150

paella, seafood 36
pan con tomate 63
pancakes
  buttermilk pancakes 199
  galettes saucisses 197
pancetta and rosemary
    pizzette 188
panzanella, grilled 90
Parmesan, roast radishes
    with crumbled 102
parsley

chimichurri 128
salsa verde 129
sepia a la plancha 84
tabbouleh 106
pasta: mac 'n' cheese 99
pavlova, lemon sherbet 176
peanuts: chicken satay 60
peppers
   chickpea, roast pepper
      and chorizo salad 109
   dirty Romesco sauce 149
   grilled panzanella 90
   huevos rancheros with
      chorizo 191
   seafood paella 36
pickles
   pickled apples 140
   pickled fennel 25
   pickled green chillies 126
   pickled red cabbage 44
   pickled vegetables 53
   pink pickled onions 126
pico de gallo with charred
   corn 123
pig cheeks, Szechuan
   smoked 26
pineapple: grilled pineapple
   with toasted brioche 180
pizza, 'nduja 54
pizzette, brunch 188
plum ketchup 26
polenta: grilled polenta with
   rosemary and Taleggio 38
pork 15
   bourbon-glazed baby back
      ribs 50
   dirty chops with rosemary
      butter and pickled fennel 25
   porchetta 30
   pork banh mi 53
   pork loin with pickled
      apples 140
   pork souvlaki 57
   pulled pork 142
   smoked pork beans on toast 195
   sticky chilli pork belly with rice
      noodle salad 28
potatoes
   baked cheese with Ratte
      potatoes 39
   Galician octopus 66
   new potatoes baked in a bag 114
   potato rolls 115

tuna niçoise as it should be 74
ultimate potato salad 104
praline: salted chocolate
   praline s'mores 183
prawns
   prawns and scallops with
      chilli and lime 70
   seafood paella 36
   smoked tiger prawns with
      dirty Romesco sauce 149
punch, rum 162

radishes
   roast radishes with crumbled
      Parmesan 102
   smoked chicken salad 146
rice: seafood paella 36
rice noodle salad 28
roasting trays 15
rocket: chickpea, roast pepper
   and chorizo salad 109
rolls, potato 115
Romesco sauce, dirty 149
rosemary
   grilled polenta with rosemary
      and Taleggio 38
   pancetta and rosemary
      pizzette 188
   rosemary butter 25
rum
   corn 'n' oil 162
   daiquiri 162
   grilled pineapple with
      toasted brioche 180
   rum punch 162
rye whisky: trois pommes 164

salads
   chargrilled leaves with
      burnt lemon dressing 94
   chickpea, roast pepper
      and chorizo salad 109
   chipotle slaw 101
   fennel salad 78
   Greek salad 110
   grilled panzanella 90
   onion salad 137
   rice noodle salad 28
   root vegetable slaw 18
   seaweed and mushroom
      salad 81
   smoked chicken salad 146
   tabbouleh 106

tuna niçoise as it should be 74
ultimate potato salad 104
salmon
   hot-smoked salmon with
      scrambled eggs 194
   smoked salmon 153
   teriyaki salmon 80
salsa
   blackened tomato salsa 122
   pico de gallo with charred
      corn 123
salsa verde 129
salt
   chicken and salt 34
   chilli and garlic salt 83
   citrus salt 83
   salted caramel ice cream 172
   salted chocolate praline
      s'mores 183
   smoked sea salt 152
   squid with three salts 83
   Szechuan seaweed salt 83
sandwiches: pork banh mi 53
satay, chicken 60
saucepans 15
sauces
   aubergine and tomato sauce 38
   béarnaise sauce 131
   chimichurri 128
   dirty Romesco sauce 149
   hollandaise sauce 192
   hot sauce 128
   mayonnaise 131
   plum ketchup 26
   quick sharp barbecue sauce 128
   salsa verde 129
   sesame aioli 53
   smoky bourbon sauce 129
   sweet chilli sauce 123
sausages
   baked eggs with merguez 190
   cheese and bacon dogs 47
   chilli dogs 48
   galettes saucisses 197
scallops
   coal-roast scallops with sweet-
      corn and Serrano ham 73
   prawns and scallops with
      chilli and lime 70
sea bass
   coal-roast sea bass with
      mussels 86
   sea bass, Ibiza style 78

sea bream: tandoori sea bream
  with chopped kachumba 77
seafood
  coal-roast scallops with sweet-
    corn and Serrano ham 73
  coal-roast sea bass with
    mussels 86
  Galician octopus 66
  lobster benedict 192
  lobster rolls 87
  prawns and scallops with
    chilli and lime 70
  seafood paella 36
  sepia a la plancha 84
  smoked tiger prawns with
    dirty Romesco sauce 149
  squid with three salts 83
seaweed
  seaweed and mushroom salad 81
  Szechuan seaweed salt 83
sepia a la plancha 84
Serrano ham, coal-roast scallops
  with sweetcorn and 73
sesame aioli 53
shawarma, lamb 137
sherbet: lemon sherbet
  pavlova 176
shish kebabs, lamb 44
slaws
  chipotle slaw 101
  root vegetable slaw 18
smokers, types of 8
smoking
  cold smoking 12
  hot smoking 11
smoky bourbon sauce 129
s'mores, salted chocolate
  praline 183
sorbet: colonel 175
sourdough bread
  smoked bone marrow
    on toast 144
  smoked chicken salad 146
souvlaki, pork 57
spray bottles 15
squid
  seafood paella 36
  squid with three salts 83
starters, chimney 11, 15
sweet chilli sauce 123
sweetcorn
  charred corn with smoked
    chilli butter 93

coal-roast scallops with sweetcorn and Serrano ham 73
pico de gallo with charred
  corn 123
Szechuan peppercorns
  Szechuan seaweed salt 83
  Szechuan smoked pig
    cheeks 26

tabbouleh 106
tacos, chipotle steak 46
tahini: yogurt and tahini
  dressing 96
Taleggio, grilled polenta
  with rosemary and 38
tandoori sea bream with
  chopped kachumba 77
tarragon: béarnaise sauce 131
temperatures, meat 15
tequila
  margarita de remolacha 160
  margarita de toronja
    picante 160
teriyaki salmon 80
Thai sweet basil: rice noodle
  salad 28
thermometers, digital probe 15
thyme butter 150
toast
  smoked bone marrow on
    toast 144
  smoked pork beans on toast 195
toffee apple ice cream 174
tomahawk steaks with blue
  cheese butter 22
tomato ketchup: quick sharp
  barbecue sauce 128
tomatoes
  aubergine and tomato sauce 38
  baked eggs with merguez 190
  blackened tomato salsa 122
  brunch pizzette 188
  dirty Romesco sauce 149
  feta and chilli parcels with
    Greek salad 110
  grilled panzanella 90
  huevos rancheros with
    chorizo 191
  kachumba 77
  'nduja pizza 54
  pan con tomate 63
  smoked chicken salad 146
  smoked pork beans on toast 195

smoked tomatoes with lardo
  di Colonnata 139
tabbouleh 106
trays, roasting 15
trois pommes 164
tuna niçoise as it should be 74
turkey 15
tzatziki 122

vanilla
  roast cherries with vanilla 182
  vanilla cream 180
vegetables
  pickled vegetables 53
  root vegetable slaw 18
  see also carrots; potatoes, etc
Velvet Falernum: corn 'n' oil 162
vodka
  colonel 175
  smoked espresso martini 166
  smoked vodka 166

wakame seaweed
  seaweed and mushroom salad 81
  Szechuan seaweed salt 83
wood, types of 12

yogurt
  tandoori sea bream with
    chopped kachumba 77
  tzatziki 122
  yogurt and tahini dressing 96

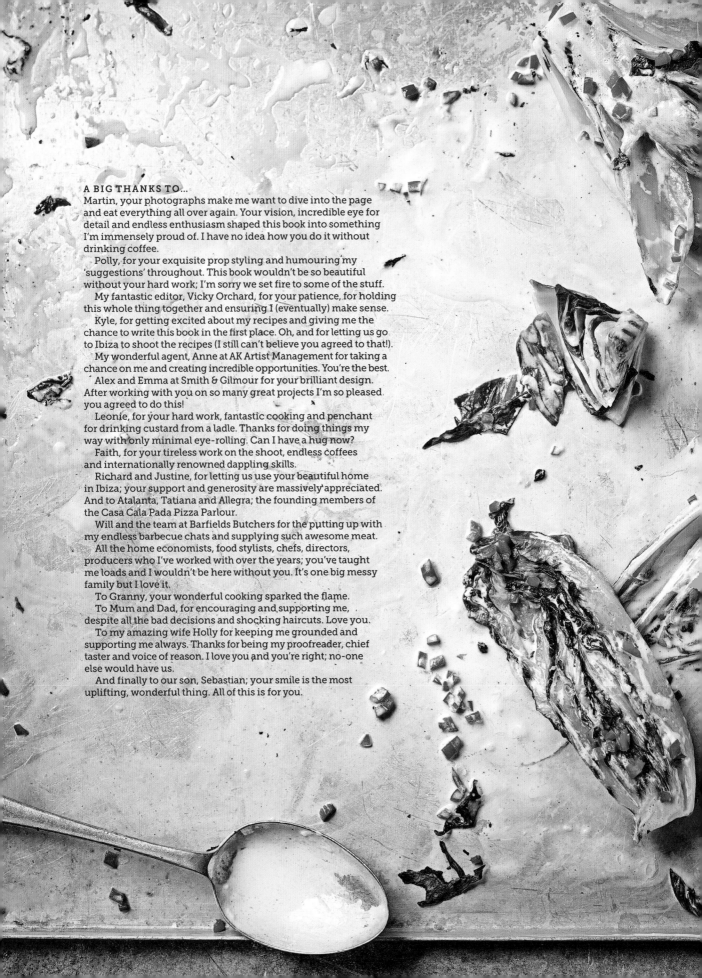

A BIG THANKS TO...

Martin, your photographs make me want to dive into the page and eat everything all over again. Your vision, incredible eye for detail and endless enthusiasm shaped this book into something I'm immensely proud of. I have no idea how you do it without drinking coffee.

Polly, for your exquisite prop styling and humouring my 'suggestions' throughout. This book wouldn't be so beautiful without your hard work; I'm sorry we set fire to some of the stuff.

My fantastic editor, Vicky Orchard, for your patience, for holding this whole thing together and ensuring I (eventually) make sense.

Kyle, for getting excited about my recipes and giving me the chance to write this book in the first place. Oh, and for letting us go to Ibiza to shoot the recipes (I still can't believe you agreed to that!).

My wonderful agent, Anne at AK Artist Management for taking a chance on me and creating incredible opportunities. You're the best.

Alex and Emma at Smith & Gilmour for your brilliant design. After working with you on so many great projects I'm so pleased you agreed to do this!

Leonie, for your hard work, fantastic cooking and penchant for drinking custard from a ladle. Thanks for doing things my way with only minimal eye-rolling. Can I have a hug now?

Faith, for your tireless work on the shoot, endless coffees and internationally renowned dappling skills.

Richard and Justine, for letting us use your beautiful home in Ibiza; your support and generosity are massively appreciated. And to Atalanta, Tatiana and Allegra; the founding members of the Casa Cala Pada Pizza Parlour.

Will and the team at Barfields Butchers for the putting up with my endless barbecue chats and supplying such awesome meat.

All the home economists, food stylists, chefs, directors, producers who I've worked with over the years; you've taught me loads and I wouldn't be here without you. It's one big messy family but I love it.

To Granny, your wonderful cooking sparked the flame.

To Mum and Dad, for encouraging and supporting me, despite all the bad decisions and shocking haircuts. Love you.

To my amazing wife Holly for keeping me grounded and supporting me always. Thanks for being my proofreader, chief taster and voice of reason. I love you and you're right; no-one else would have us.

And finally to our son, Sebastian; your smile is the most uplifting, wonderful thing. All of this is for you.